PERSONAL TUTORING IN HIGHER EDUCATION

PERSONAL TUTORING IN HIGHER EDUCATION

Edited by
Liz Thomas and Paula Hixenbaugh

Trentham Books
Stoke on Trent, UK and Sterling, USA

Trentham Books Limited
Westview House   22883 Quicksilver Drive
734 London Road   Sterling
Oakhill   VA 20166-2012
Stoke on Trent   USA
Staffordshire
England ST4 5NP

First published 2006

British Library Cataloguing-in-Publication Data
A catalogue record for this book is available from the British Library

ISBN-13: 978-1-85856-385-5
ISBN-10: 1-85856-385-2

Designed and typeset by Trentham Print Design Ltd, Chester and
printed in Great Britain by Bemrose Shafron (Printers) Ltd, Chester.

Contents

Notes on contributors

Sheila Aynsley-Smith has been Head of Student Services at Manchester Metropolitan University since 1995 and manages student support services across the University's campuses. Sheila sits on the AUA (Association of University Administrators) Executive, the Editorial Advisory Board for *Perspectives* (the AUA journal) and the CPD Advisory Committee. She co-ordinates the mentoring scheme for the Association of Managers of Student Services in higher education and regularly presents sessions at both Association of Managers of Student Services in Higher Education (AMOSSHE) and AUA conferences. Sheila is a Governor of a community school with Language and Training College Status.

Ruth Barrett is a Principal Lecturer in Computer Science at the University of Hertfordshire and programme tutor for an online masters course, with experience of personal tutoring for both distance students and on-campus students and extensive experience of pastoral care.

Margo Blythman is director of teaching and learning at the London College of Communication, University of the Arts, London. Her responsibilities include staff development, the quality of teaching and learning, tutorial systems and study support. She has published with Susan Orr on such topics as retention, development strategies within higher education contexts and the development of student academic writing, particularly in the context of art and design. Her academic interests also include the impact of quality assurance systems on the working lives of academic staff and micropolitics in UK higher education.

Rosalind Crouch is a Principal Lecturer in Computer Science at the University of Hertfordshire, with extensive experience of personal tutoring and pastoral care. She is a member of the Universities UK/Standing Committee of Principals (UUK/ SCOP) Committee for the Promotion of Mental Well Being in Higher Education and is currently involved in preparing guidelines on Mental Health Promotion in HE.

Crispin P L Farbrother is the Programme Leader for the undergraduate Hospitality programmes in the School of Services Management at Bournemouth University. These are successful programmes recently coming top in the Guardian and second in the *Times'* league tables. He specialises in Strategic Management and Marketing. Crispin is the Institutional Representative for the Higher Education Academy's Hospitality Leisure, Sport and Tourism Subject Network and was recently appointed to sit on its Advisory Panel. Crispin is also an Executive Committee member of the Council for Hospitality Management in Education. His research and consultancy interests are in food services management, international marketing and personal tutoring.

Annie Grant is currently the Dean of Students at the University of East Anglia (UEA), a role that includes overall responsibility for the University's Careers Centre and a wide range of other student services. Her early career was as an academic archaeologist in a number of UK Higher Education institutions. In 1991 she moved to the University of Leicester, first as Director of their Enterprise Learning Initiative and then as the Director of the Educational Development and Support Centre. She moved to her current post at UEA in 2004.

Daphne Hampton is a senior lecturer at the London College of Communication, University of the Arts, London. She is the student mentor co-ordinator for the college, a member of the study support team and tutorial co-ordinator for the Marketing School. She combines research into student mentoring with the practical experience of running student mentoring schemes over several years and has acted as a consultant in this field. Her research interests are student mentoring and the first year student experience on foundation degrees: she has published in these areas.

Heather Hartwell is a senior lecturer in the School of Services Management at Bournemouth University specialising in Nutrition and Food Safety. She is first year tutor, Peer Assisted Learning contact and was instrumental in introducing *Stepping Stones* to the hospitality programmes. Heather delivers courses for both the Institution of Environmental Health Officers and for the Royal Society for the Promotion of Health, where she is also a member of the editorial board of the Society's journal, recently leading a specialist issue *Hospitality and Health*. Research and consultancy interests are in hospital food service and personal tutoring.

Peter Hill is Principal Lecturer in Marketing and a Teaching Fellow at the University of Westminster where he has led a number of large undergraduate courses. His life is otherwise uninteresting.

Paula Hixenbaugh is a Principal Lecturer in Psychology at the University of Westminster. She is the Regent Campus Senior Tutor, responsible for co-ordinating personal tutoring across the campus. For the last 30 years she has lectured and researched across a wide range of areas in psychology. She is qualified as a chartered counselling psychologist and also has experience in private counselling practice. Her research focuses on the student experience. She is currently chair of a research group studying the first year experience and factors leading to student success.

Barbara Lee is Reader in Learning and Teaching for Southampton Business School at Southampton Solent University and is involved in the development of careers education in the curriculum. Her research interests focus on academic literacy and in students learning to create and structure legal argument.

Liz Marr is a Principal Lecturer in the Department of Sociology at Manchester Metropolitan University and Head of Widening Participation (WP), in the Faculty of Humanities, Law and Social Science. In addition to research into and dissemination of best practice relating to WP and retention, she is actively involved in the development of employability, across the range of the faculty's courses. Other responsibilities include the implementation of student support systems, co-ordination of diversity initiatives and the development of personal development planning.

Martina McLaughlin is a Senior Lecturer at the London College of Communication, University of the Arts, London. Her responsibilities include lecturing in Media Theory on undergraduate and postgraduate courses in the Journalism department. She is also tutorial co-ordinator which is a shared post for the Media School. She has delivered conference presentations on journalism and popular culture and the role of the tutorial co-ordinator in higher education. Her academic interests include working in higher education as a personal tutor on the history of journalism.

Susan Orr was previously Teaching and Learning Co-ordinator at the London College of Fashion, University of the Arts, London. She is currently a Principal Lecturer for Quality Management and Enhancement at the School of Arts at York St John College. She is responsible for developing and implementing strategies to improve the quality of the students' learning experience. Susan is a published researcher whose work focuses on higher education pedagogy. Her interests include assessment as a social practice, students' approaches to textual and visual assessment and widening participation. She has presented papers at a number of conferences in the UK, Europe and the USA and has co-authored a range of articles, papers and chapters with Margo Blythman.

Carol Pearson is a Senior lecturer in Psychology at the University of Westminster. Her teaching interests are in Social and Critical Psychology. Her research focuses on aspects of teaching and learning in higher education, including student expectations and achievements predictors, student progression and social and academic integration. Recently she has focused on both first year and minority group undergraduate students' experiences in higher education. Carol specialises in qualitative research methodology.

Charlotte Ramage is a Principal Lecturer at the Institute of Nursing and Midwifery, Brighton University. She is a work-based learning framework co-ordinator, which has generated her interest in reflection and how people learn through work. She has written various chapters and journal articles that reflect these areas of interest. Her recent research has focused on generating an understanding of the roles of those involved in work-based learning.

Pauline Ridley is a member of the University of Brighton's Centre for Learning and Teaching which supports all aspects of the work of academic staff. She contributes to their courses, events and the development of online and print resources, including guidance for new personal tutors. She has previously worked in the LTSN (now the Higher Education Academy) Subject Centre for Art Design Media and is also involved in Brighton's new Centres of Excellence in Teaching and Learning, particularly as Visual Practices learning area co-ordinator for the Learn Higher CETL consortium.

Alan Robinson is the Associate Dean (Academic Operations), for the Faculty of Technology at Southampton Solent University. His research interests include the development of aligned learning, teaching and assessment strategies to aid retention, promote independent learning and enhance student achievement.

Ormond Simpson is Senior Lecturer in the Centre for Institutional Research, Institute of Educational Technology, Open University (OU), where his main interests are researching into student retention, widening participation and the implications of movements towards e-learning. Before that appointment he worked in student support in the OU for 25 years, having previously worked in universities in Africa and the US. He is the author of many articles on student support and retention and of two books, *Supporting Students in Online, Open and Distance Learning* and *Student Retention in Online, Open and Distance Learning*, both with RoutledgeFalmer.

Liz Thomas is Senior Adviser for Widening Participation at the Higher Education Academy. She is actively involved in research, policy and practice related to widening participation and improving students' learning experiences. Liz is particularly interested in the retention and success of students from under-represented groups and in institutional change to support this. She has managed and participated in national, and international research projects on these and related issues. She is co-editor of the peer-reviewed journal *Widening Participation and Lifelong Learning* and a member of the editorial boards of *Higher Education Quarterly* and the *Journal of Access Policy and Practice*.

Harry Waterworth is Senior Lecturer at the School of Printing and Publishing at the London College of Communication, University of the Arts, London. His roles include tutorial co-ordinator, admissions tutor co-ordinator, AP(E)L advisor and director of undergraduate on-line learning. He has worked both here and abroad with government agencies to establish new colleges, train staff in the use of technology for production and teaching methodology together with education quality management systems. This has provided insight into the needs, wants and aspirations of international students. He has used this experience to establish strong personal tutorial provision within the school.

Dave Williams is a Lecturer at the University of Westminster, where he gained his PhD in October 2003 which investigated the effects of emotionally valenced environmental information on the perception of pain stimuli. His main areas of teaching are Research Methods, Psychobiology and Health Psychology. He has broad teaching experience and has produced written teaching materials for the Open University, developed and delivered courses nationally for the NHS University to senior health workers and has developed and delivered a training course for the Team Health Project for Haringey NHS Trust and for Pfeizer Health Solutions.

Sally Wootton is Tutorial Manager at Wakefield College and has extensive experience of tutorial support and development in both further and higher education. Her research interests include tutorial policy and practice, mentoring strategies in education and continuing professional development for personal tutors, teachers and trainers. She has contributed to a number of tutoring and mentoring publications and is currently completing her doctoral thesis, which explores students' and tutors' perspectives on personal tutoring practice and relationships. She is a member of the European Mentoring and Coaching Council, the National Mentoring and Befriending Foundation and Chair of the Northern Tutorial Network.

Section 1:
Context and current agendas

1

Introduction

Liz Thomas and Paula Hixenbaugh

Origins and purpose

This book fills a gap in the research and development of personal tutoring in higher education institutions in the UK in the 21st century. It is practically orientated and research-informed, drawing on studies and evaluated interventions from a range of institutions and contexts. A review of literature has confirmed that there is little published material explicitly about personal tutoring, and that much of what does exist is out of date and does not reflect the current UK context of increasing student numbers, worsening staff/student ratios, greater student diversity, competing demands on staff in relation to research, learning and teaching, student support and guidance and administrative responsibilities and new modes and sites of higher education (HE) delivery.

The book arose out of an identified need by colleagues engaged in personal tutoring and related activities across the sector. Staff were investigating, developing and implementing alternative approaches to student support in their institutions in response to the changing higher education landscape and the pressure to ensure high rates of student retention and success. Many staff felt isolated and unrecognised in their institutions, and were eager for networking to gain support and external information, research and evaluation evidence to inform their work.

The first national conference on personal tutoring was organised by the Higher Education Academy and the University of Westminster in May 2005. The event confirmed the importance of the topic and the extent of activity and change taking place in the sector. This book draws together current research, investigation and evaluation about personal tutoring and student support to:

- inform and develop conceptual understandings of the issues
- provide evidence of the renewed need for personal tutoring in all types of higher education institutions
- present the financial case for re-introducing or improving personal tutoring systems
- gain insight into student perceptions of personal tutoring and how it could be improved
- offer evaluated examples of how UK institutions have overhauled their personal tutoring systems and the advantages and implications of these approaches
- consider how to bring about institutional change
- identify staff perceptions, experiences and support needs in relation to tutoring
- examine tutoring via different modes of delivery, particularly online learning, and the implications for staff
- explore how the role of tutors is changing in different contexts, particularly in relation to work-based learning.

Consequently this book will prove a particularly useful resource for staff with responsibility for improving student retention and success, personal tutoring systems and student support. It provides practical, evidence-informed approaches to overcoming current challenges. We anticipate that it will also be of interest and value to senior staff with a broader remit to enhance students' learning experiences, to staff engaged in personal tutoring and student support, those involved in widening participation activities and to researchers with an interest in personal tutoring and related areas such as learning, teaching and student success.

Overview of the book

The book is organised into three sections:

- context and current agendas
- institutional models and approaches
- issues and implications for staff

4

Section 1: Context and current agendas

The first section reviews the current context of personal tutoring and the higher education environment in the UK. In summary, research evidence is used to argue the case for personal tutoring in all types of institutions and to consider the different roles and purposes offered by personal tutoring and how alternative models and approaches to tutoring can meet emerging needs. Compelling evidence is presented about the positive financial implications of tutoring for institutions and the section concludes by considering what students want from personal tutoring systems.

Annie Grant provides a brief history of personal tutoring in the UK and reviews the challenges that many HEIs now face in organising and maintaining traditional personal tutoring systems. Drawing on research in two research-intensive universities, she outlines the significant contribution that a robust personal tutor system can make, but at the same time questions the need for departmentally-based personal support in the light of the expansion and development of central student services over the last two decades. Accordingly, she argues for the development of much stronger relationships between departmental personal tutor systems and central student services to enhance provision for students, reduce the burden on staff and maximise the use of institutional resources. In this way the benefits of personal tutoring can be preserved and the system need not be perceived as in crisis but rather in need of reform.

Liz Thomas explores the potential role of personal tutoring within the context of mass higher education and greater student diversity as a consequence of widening participation. She identifies the different roles personal tutoring can play: provision of information about higher education processes, procedures and expectations; academic feedback and development; personal welfare support; referral to further information and support and a relationship with the institution and a sense of belonging. Drawing from the literature, she reviews the different models of personal tutoring: pastoral approaches, professional models and integrated curriculum designs. Based on UK-wide qualitative research with first generation entrants and working class students who withdrew from post-1992 higher education institutions, she uses two students' experiences to explore how an integrated personal tutoring strategy could have benefited these students and perhaps prevented them from leaving higher education. She concludes that the challenge for many institutions is how to develop a time and cost-effective integrated and proactive personal tutoring system which benefits all students.

Having established the case for personal tutoring from a learning and teaching perspective in the previous chapters, Ormond Simpson uses experiences at the Open University in the UK to assess the financial costs and benefits of personal tutoring. The University abolished its personal tutoring system, which appears to have been related to a decrease in student retention and progression. This presented an opportunity to experiment with the re-introduction of personal tutoring and to assess the costs and benefits. In summary this revealed that the average cost of additional contact with students was £200 and that this resulted in increasing retention rates by 5 per cent, with a saving of £1300 per student, which represents a 550 per cent return on investment. Ormond therefore argues that re-introducing a personal tutoring system is a sound financial decision on the part of the institution, especially in the changing climate of increased student fees, where students may be looking for a good return on their investment – and a lower risk of withdrawal.

The section concludes by exploring students' perceptions and expectations of personal tutoring. Paula Hixenbaugh and colleagues at the University of Westminster note the importance of personal tutoring but also the fact that there is little research on what students actually want from a personal tutoring system. In this chapter they focus on the findings from research with students at the university about personal tutoring. While students are generally satisfied with the personal tutoring provision, they are able to evaluate it critically, and make concrete suggestions for improvement. What emerges is that relationships are central to students' higher education experience and that personal tutors can play an important role in enhancing academic relations. Students therefore want a more proactive and structured approach to personal tutoring.

This section therefore provides a clear message and research base that personal tutoring is highly desirable in the 21st century but that it needs to be reformed. It is no longer feasible to sustain traditional models of tutoring but new models are required. This may include approaches which are integrated into the curriculum, so bringing together academic and professional support; they must reach all students, not just those who voluntarily access tutors and/or student services.

Section 2: Institutional models and approaches
The second section of the book considers different ways in which higher education institutions in the UK have developed personal tutoring strategies to better support their students to be successful in mass higher education. It is apparent that these innovations resonate with and support the conclusions

drawn from the previous section about the type of reforms required. Each of these interventions is described within its institutional context and critically evaluated using institutional data and research. This section therefore offers invaluable insights and evidence to support institutional change in other universities and colleges.

Heather Hartwell and Crispin Farbrother discuss how they have used personal tutoring to enhance the first year experience and improve student progression and retention at Bournemouth University, where tutoring has been used as a space to offer students a sense of security and to demonstrate that the institution cares about their well-being. The initial pilot resulted in the development of a curriculum-based model of tutoring to develop students' understanding of higher education and to facilitate integration into their programmes of study. The new induction and tutoring programme starts prior to entry and extends into the first year. The authors report on the research and evaluation underpinning this work, as well as the intervention itself.

At Manchester Metropolitan University, Sheila Aynsley-Smith and Liz Marr were also faced with the need to develop an alternative model of delivery of academic and pastoral student support for a large and diverse student population. They sought to join up support provided by academic and student services staff to provide seamless provision. The approach used was the creation of Student Support Officers (SSOs) within faculties. Following a successful pilot in 2003, the SSO system was rolled out across the university in 2005. The SSOs provide localised support to students within their faculties, bridging the gap between the delivery of support locally by academic and personal tutors and centrally by specialist student services. The authors provide a detailed outline of the system, looking at the context in which the need for the system was identified, the role of the SSOs and some of the advantages of the system over the more *ad hoc* personal tutoring system.

Barbara Lee and Alan Robinson also wanted to develop an integrated and holistic system of student support at Southampton Solent University. Their research identified that students want to manage their support network, to understand fully how to access services when they need them and to choose the most appropriate person to support them at that time. The institution has therefore developed an approach in which academic and support staff work together to deliver an effective network of student support. The authors begin by reviewing the original system for student support, before going on to discuss the drivers and founding principles behind the development of the Student Support Network, Students 1st system and the Spiral Induction Programme (SIP). They conclude with an evaluation of the impact and success of some of the work.

The focus of Peter Hill's chapter is on the creation of peer support networks amongst a large and diverse undergraduate population within the Business School at the University of Westminster. Observation and subsequent analysis revealed that many students had limited opportunities for meeting the same peers in course seminars, which reduced their ability to make friends and feel socially engaged in the learning environment. The situation is further compounded by external commitments such as paid employment and family responsibilities that take students away from the university. This chapter explores these issues and the implementation of platoons that group students together for seminars, which increases their social interaction and reduces isolation and student withdrawal.

In the final chapter in this section, Margo Blythman and colleagues (2002) take a longer term and more strategic view of change by analysing their experience of developing a new approach to tutoring over the last nine years at the University of the Arts, London. The authors provide an account of the way in which personal tutoring structures and cultures have developed, focusing particularly on the role of the tutorial coordinator. Furthermore, they look at the ways in which these developments relate to the university's and its constituent colleges' wider structures and aims, and some of the problems encountered in these developments. In addition, seeking to highlight the benefit of deeper theoretical understanding of educational issues on the success of personal tutorial systems, Blythman and Orr situate their experience and a strategic approach to tutoring within a discussion of the concepts of cultural capital, 'the space between', access and participation, academic literacies and micropolitics. Within this theoretical perspective they conclude by providing recommendations for those trying to develop and implement tutorial systems in their own institutions.

Section 3: Issues and implications for staff
The final section of the book highlights issues in personal tutoring which are of particular relevance to staff. Sally Wootton discusses the greater complexity of needs that a more diverse group of students are bringing to personal tutoring. Yet the exact role of the personal tutor is often not specified within institutions, leaving the tutor to fall back on 'a variety of misguided historical practices'. Sally reports on the results of her investigation on student and staff perceptions of personal tutoring which lead her to argue for the importance of

placing personal tutoring at the centre of the learning experience. She describes personal tutoring as a core activity, linking student services and curriculum support, and calls on the higher education community to develop professional standards and competencies for the tutoring role.

The diversity of the tutoring role and the pressures felt by staff are themes discussed by Pauline Ridley. She focuses on the perceptions, experiences and well being of personal tutors and describes developments at the University of Brighton to improve the support offered to personal tutors. Pauline has found that many new staff have difficulty setting boundaries and can feel overwhelmed by students' needs. In the context of increasing workloads for all higher education staff, personal tutors can be left feeling unsupported. Pauline describes a personal tutoring guide which encourages tutors to set boundaries and to develop their own personal tutoring style. However, the need for peer support is emphasised as an important buffer against the stresses of this demanding but rewarding role.

New models of personal tutoring are developing and Rosalind Crouch and Ruth Barrett discuss online tutoring at the University of Hertfordshire. They investigated staff experiences in building relationships with students online and whether it was possible to meet students' personal and study problems without face-to-face contact. While staff saw advantages to an online environment, they felt that it was difficult to deal with personal tutoring issues entirely online. Rosalind and Ruth discuss a range of verbal and non-verbal strategies that may help to overcome some of these difficulties. Like Pauline Ridley in the previous chapter, they highlight the need for support for tutors so they can carry out their role effectively. They argue that specific training for tutors involved in online personal tutoring is necessary, as well as the provision of accessible institutional student support services.

In the final chapter Charlotte Ramage uses a qualitative, grounded theory approach to explore how learners are supported in the workplace in the health sector. She considers how learners, staff and mentors need to adapt their role to suit this context, which is very different to a traditional higher education learning environment. In particular, she focuses on the lack of structure the workplace appears to offer to learning and ways in which tutors, or educational advisers, need to support the process of creating structure and support, especially through learning contracts, action learning to keep the learner on track, and guiding learning in the work context. This chapter highlights the changing roles for academic staff as new approaches to, and modes of delivery of learning become more commonplace in the mass higher education sector.

This section therefore reinforces the central argument of this book, that personal tutoring needs to be integrated into students' learning experience, wherever and however the learning takes place. For this to happen, staff need appropriate guidance, training and support to enable them to fulfil new personal tutoring roles within changed institutional systems and higher education environments.

2

Personal tutoring:
A system in crisis?

Annie Grant

Introduction

C hanges in UK higher education policy over the last ten and more years have had a significant impact on the size, diversity, and expectations of the UK student body and at the same time increased the demands placed on higher education (HE) staff. An effective personal tutor system is demanding of staff time, commitment and skills, yet the system survives in a significant proportion of UK higher education institutions (HEIs), and in particular in the pre-1992 sector. The focus of this chapter is the traditional personal tutor/advisor system delivered by departmentally-based academic staff. It draws on the authors' work in two research intensive institutions, the Universities of East Anglia (UEA) and Leicester, including research undertaken at the latter as part of a project to enhance provision for students with mental health difficulties (The Student Psychological Health Project, SPHP). As part of this project an extensive questionnaire was administered to large cohorts of second year undergraduates in 1998 and again in 2001; the survey included a number of questions on students' help-seeking behaviour (Grant, 2002). Additional data on students' views of the tutorial system is drawn from the results of the University of Leicester's *Graduate Survey for 2001*, which sought feedback from finalists on their student experience.

This chapter looks at the development of undergraduate personal advice and guidance systems in the UK and the challenges that many HEIs are now facing in organising and maintaining these functions. It outlines the significant contribution that a robust personal tutor system can make but also questions the need for departmentally-based personal support in the light of the expansion and development of central student services over the last two decades. Finally the author argues the case for the development of much stronger relationships between departmental personal tutor systems and central student services as a way of enhancing provision and at the same time maximising the use of institutional resources.

Background

One of the key drivers for the early development of the personal tutorial system in the UK is a longstanding tradition, particularly strong in England, but much less so in Scotland, Ireland and Wales, for students to go away to university rather than to attend one near home. Until 1970, young people did not become legally adult until they were 21; universities were thus responsible not only for academic provision but also for the well being of their young students: they were legally *in loco parentis* for their resident under 21 year-olds. In Oxford and Cambridge, and other collegiate institutions developed on their model, moral tutors, who were also teaching and research staff, offered personal guidance and support to a small group of students within their college. Academic guidance was the responsibility of directors of study; an important principle of separation of academic from non-academic personal guidance underpinned this division of responsibilities.

Departmental personal tutors were also part of the non-collegiate universities founded from the late 19th century through to the second half of the 20th century. In many of which an additional element of student support was provided in halls of residence by a warden, also a member of academic staff, who took on responsibility for the welfare of the students in their hall of residence.

Some of the centralised student services, now a feature of all UK HEIs, also have a relatively long history: the earliest careers services – those at Oxford and Cambridge – were established in 1892 and 1902 respectively and the first university counselling service was established in Leicester in 1946 (Swainson, 1977). These services were developed to provide more professional advice and counselling than could be offered by academic staff whose primary role and skills were in research and teaching. In the last two decades a much wider range of centralised provision has developed: most institutions now offer not only careers advice and guidance and personal counselling but also financial advice, support for students with disabilities and specific learning difficulties, academic learning and skills development and faith guidance; Grant (in press, a) discusses the development and scope of central student service provision in the UK in more detail.

A system in crisis?

In the current climate, providing an effective departmentally-based personal tutor or adviser system presents a range of challenges that were not encountered when the system was first developed within an elite higher education system. Widening participation initiatives and international recruitment has created a student body that is very diverse in age, background, nationality and ethnicity. Many students experience personal difficulties and face practical problems whose resolution requires more specialised knowledge, experience and skills than the average departmental staff member could reasonably be expected to offer.

A decline in per capita funding for undergraduate teaching has worsened staff/student ratios, making it more difficult for academic staff to get to know their tutees. At the University of Nottingham academic staff reported that they knew their students less well than in the past and cited increased pressure on time and increasing student numbers as the cause (Grant and Woolfson, 2001). Getting to know students is even more difficult where modular degree programmes allow them to study courses offered across a number of different academic departments or units. Many academic staff are committed in principle to a personal tutor system and see their role as a tutor as one of the most rewarding aspects of teaching. However, because of increasing pressure to research and undertake administrative tasks, there is also staff resistance to personal tutoring of a non-academic nature.

At an institutional level there is the challenge of ensuring consistency of practice. Staff/student ratios vary in different subject areas: typically, ratios are worse in arts and humanities subjects than in the sciences. Not all academics are naturally suited to an advisory role or are prepared to commit to one. Excusing some staff their personal tutor responsibilities places additional pressure on others. Some institutions therefore ask all teaching staff to take on the personal tutor role for a group of students, and try to enhance advisory skills though appropriate training. However, academics are notoriously resistant to staff development: take-up is frequently low.

Is a robust and effective personal tutor system delivered by academic staff any longer achievable? And with the growth of multi-professional central services in many institutions, is it even necessary? There might be a strong argument for leaving lecturing staff to teach and guide students academically and for student services staff to deliver professional personal and practical support.

However, this view has not been taken by the majority of HEIs. Data obtained from a recent postal survey, undertaken by the Universities UK (UUK) Committee for the Promotion of Mental Well-being in Higher Education, indicated that some form of compulsory personal tutor system remains the norm, particularly in pre-1992 institutions, specialist institutions and colleges of higher education (Table 1). Indeed both my current and previous institutions are re-iterating their commitment to a traditional personal tutor/advisor system and have reviewed and developed institutional guidelines, setting down minimum requirements for frequency of student/adviser contact and adviser availability.

Table 1: percentage of HEIs with a compulsory personal tutor system in place (N = 78, response rate 50%. Source: Grant (in press b))

Institution type	Pre-1992	Post-1992	Specialist/College of HE	All
%	86	43	91	74

The roles of the personal tutor

A brief paper, published in 1999 by Tony Watts, offered an analysis of the role of the personal adviser in the context of government strategies on post-compulsory schooling and social exclusion. Although the discussion did not specifically address higher education, the paper's distillation of the key roles for an adviser can be adapted as a benchmark or reference point against which to judge the effectiveness of HE guidance or advisory provision. They are:

■ providing ongoing support based on an established relationship
■ providing holistic guidance, that is encompassing academic and personal, information, advice and guidance
■ referral to other specialist agencies
■ advocacy *via* references and representation (adapted from Watts, 1999, p3).

The first role emphasises continuity of contact. Departmentally-based tutors can offer advice and guidance within a student's everyday learning environment where there are naturally occurring opportunities to build up a relationship gradually through casual as well as teaching contact. This encourages the development of relationships of trust and confidence which are essential if students are to talk freely about personal or academic difficulties they may be facing. The importance of frequent contact in establishing these trusting relationships can be inferred from students' responses to questions in the Leicester SPHP survey, which asked where they went when they needed help or advice (Table 2). They were more likely to turn to their personal tutor and to others in their day-to-day world than to consult the specialist services, even when they are well promoted and highly rated by those who use them, as at this university. Students may only rarely come into contact with central services staff on a casual basis and may therefore be reluctant or unwilling to seek advice outside their familiar circles. The survey indicated that students were as likely to turn to their personal tutors and/or other departmentally-based staff as they were to consult the counselling service for help with psychological problems.

Table 2: students' help-seeking behaviour (N = 2738, response rate 78%. Source: Grant, 2002)

Source of help and advice:	for all concerns (%);	for psychological problems (%)
Family and friends	66	22
Personal tutor	56	4
Other academic staff	34	2
Departmental secretaries	21	< 1
Welfare service	11	2
Counselling service	7	5

The issue of close staff-student contact was specifically addressed in the review of the departmental advisory system recently undertaken at UEA. The report of the working group that undertook the review concluded that

> an advisory system that removed from academics the primary responsibility for providing academic and pastoral advice to undergraduate students was likely to create an unnecessary, and in its opinion, unhealthy distance between faculty and students. (UEA, 2005, 2 p8)

Watt's second key role is one of holistic guidance that encompasses both the academic and personal. This is an opposite approach to that of the traditional approach of long-established collegiate institutions where each undergraduate still has a director of studies to offer guidance and feedback on academic performance and a tutor who is responsible for help with personal matters. This division is now unusual even at Cambridge: some colleges have incorporated the two roles. Such a separation has little relevance to the modern student, whose ability to study effectively is increasingly affected by their financial situation, where and with whom they are living, their relation-ships with friends and family, their social and academic background and their physical health and psychological stability.

Holistic responsibility makes the tutor more able to undertake Watt's fourth role of advocacy, particularly when it comes to writing references. There is in-creasing competition for graduate-level jobs and employers are less interested in the fine details of a student's academic achievements than they are in knowing what kind of a person the student is. They want to know whether they have taken part in voluntary or sporting activities and whether they managed to complete their coursework in time while working part time. The involvement of tutorial staff in the implementation of the personal development planning (PDP) schemes, now compulsory for HEIs, can help to encourage a broad discussion of students' achievements and aspirations and of any difficulties that are impeding their progress.

Personal tutors and other departmental staff are in a unique position for spotting a student who is experiencing difficulties at an early stage. However, they are not always best placed to offer the most effective advice and guidance. Declining academic performance may not be a symptom of academic difficulties but may indicate other more personal concerns. The in-creasing numbers of students who experience mental illness has been widely reported (Rana *et al*, 1999; Grant, 2002). Tutors may not possess the ex-perience or ability to recognise the early signs of the onset of mental illness, nor, more critically, how or where to refer students. Watt's third key role is that of referral to appropriate agencies; this is addressed below.

The increasing diversity of the student body has undoubtedly made the roles of the personal adviser and of student services more complex. Analysis of the *Leicester Graduate Survey* responses showed that personal support was more important to women than to men; it also revealed that women students in departments with few female academic staff gave lower average ratings to the quality of the advice and support which was provided than women who were in departments with a higher proportion of female staff. The SPHP survey also showed significant differences in the reported experiences of students of different age groups and from different ethnic and religious backgrounds. Shifting the ethnic or gender balance of academic staff is not a realistic short-term solution, whereas ensuring that all staff are aware of the potential im-pact of gender and cultural differences on their students' expectations and experiences of higher education is more achievable.

Personal tutors and student services

Central student services are frequently organised around a range of inter-linked professional units. While tutors may be able to help with most difficulties presented by their tutees, the resolution of complex problems needs more specialised advice, especially for practical matters such as finance or international students' visa queries, or with physical or mental health, interpersonal relationships, or if they require cultural sensitivities in areas unfamiliar to the personal tutor. Effective referral requires accurate knowledge of the full range of services available so that the tutor can encourage the student to seek additional help from the most appropriate quarter, without appearing to be passing the buck.

One of the key roles that student services can play is to be a source of neutral and confidential advice about both personal and academic issues. A significant proportion of the students that I see in my current role want to talk about an issue that they do not want either those that teach them and mark their academic work, or their friends and families, to know about. Even when their difficulty is primarily academic, they may want advice on how to approach their tutor or lecturer. Students on professional courses may be particularly concerned that their difficulties may have fitness to practice implications. The student may resolve their difficulty within this confidential environment but may ultimately require the involvement of academic staff. If this is necessary, student services staff may be able to provide a co-ordinating role or help the student feel confident and comfortable to approach their personal tutor or other departmental staff. In some cases the nature of the concerns raised may make it impossible to offer complete confidentiality (any limitations on confidentiality will be clearly explained to the student concerned) but student services staff may, with the student's permission, be able to act as an intermediary or to help the student to come to terms with their situation. Such interventions and negotiations take a considerable amount of time and the involvement of, or referral to student services can significantly reduce the burden placed on the personal tutor as well as help the student.

In other situations, the personal advisor may be happy and willing to continue to help the student but may ask for advice from student services staff on how to approach a difficult situation. The Leicester SPHP research included a survey of staff, asking them about their experiences of responding to students and the kind of training and advice that would be most helpful. Many said that they felt inadequately trained to be able to recognise students who were in more serious difficulty, or to know which of the central services were the most appropriate referral point. The responses also indicated that any guidance or training should be relevant and focused in order to take the minimum amount of time (Grant and Woolfson, 2001). An early outcome of the project was a booklet entitled *Helping Students in Difficulty*, written by student services staff and distributed widely across the institution; this was extremely well received. Further guidance was offered though workshops and briefer sessions in departmental meetings or on away days. This ensured some level of involvement even from those who will perhaps always be reluctant to go to training events. These initiatives offer a good example of the ways in which student services can work with, and support the role of the personal tutor.

The institutional perspective

It is evident that students value the pastoral/personal support offered at a departmental level: over half the respondents to the 2001 *Leicester Graduate Survey* rated it as of above average importance. It is also apparent from this survey that the quality of the support provided played a significant part in the way that the respondents felt about their overall student experience. The responses that finalists gave to the question asking them to rate their level of agreement with a statement saying *the academic staff have cared about my well-being* was positively correlated with responses to *I am proud to have been a student at this university.*

The Universities of Leicester's and East Anglia's commitment to their personal tutor/adviser systems may well have played an important part in the high ratings received from their students in the 2005 *National Student Survey*. Other factors must have contributed to the high levels of satisfaction – both institutions while having a significant commitment to, and focus on, research, also have a genuine interest in teaching and learning. Other institutional benefits of strong pastoral support systems include a positive impact on student progression, achievement and retention.

Ensuring consistency of practice will always be challenging. Student feedback on their tutors can range from *my tutor is brilliant*, to *my tutor is never there in his office hours*. Academics do not always have the most appropriate skills and commitment to guide and advise appropriately. Problems can also arise when staff become too involved in supporting their students and do not refer students on to professionally trained staff at the most appropriate point, sometimes unintentionally worsening their student's situation and causing themselves significant distress.

In my own interactions with students, sometimes when I ask if a student has discussed their concern with their tutor, the student's response is that they *didn't want to bother him as he is so busy with his research*. While we would wish students to understand the context in which they are studying and the broad range of tasks that academic staff have to undertake, they should not be deterred from seeking advice from academic staff because they fear that staff will resent being interrupted: they are entitled to this information.

There are real risks for an institution when the personal tutor system goes wrong. There may be exposure through the results of the *National Student Survey*, and individual problems may lead to damaging and time-consuming complaints and appeals and if a satisfactory resolution cannot be found, referral to the Office of the Independent Adjudicator. In an increasingly consumerist society there is much danger in offering services that do not meet the expectations and promises made about them. Clear information about what is and is not provided, who does what and when and what is expected of students can reduce the risk of disappointment and distress and help the tutor.

Conclusion

This chapter has only been able to touch the surface of many of the issues it has raised about the delivery of effective academic and personal guidance in the current HE context. Despite the challenges it presents at an institutional level and the pressures it can place on individual academic staff members, which I do not underestimate, the personal tutor system can still offer an effective way of delivering an excellent and consistent teaching and learning experience for a diverse student body. However, I argue that building stronger and institutionally supported relationships between departmental academic staff and professional staff in student services departments will significantly reduce some of the pressures experienced in maintaining a high quality provision.

My chapter has looked at one part of the current HE landscape, that inhabited by pre-1992 research intensive institutions. In HEIs where students are taught by staff who are based in several different academic units or departments, the traditional departmentally-based personal tutorial system may not be the most effective way to guide and support them. My own experiences and research do not allow me to comment with much authority in this area, although Leicester students studying joint degrees across two departments tended to give lower ratings to their satisfaction with the support that they were offered, compared with those who were studying a single subject. I question the assumption that as the proportion of students who study locally and remain in their family home increases, the need for HEIs to offer personal advice and guidance systems will decline. The SPHP research demonstrated that students who were living at home made greater demands on many of the central services than those living in university or private accommodation. This finding re-enforces the point made earlier about the value for students of having someone to turn to within their everyday environment, and being able to access advice that is neutral and confidential and unconnected to their existing personal or academic relationships.

To return to the title of this chapter, the personal tutor system need not be in crisis if it can develop and adapt in response to changing circumstances and can operate more effectively in collaboration with information, advice and guidance services provided centrally in HEIs.

3

Widening participation and the increased need for personal tutoring

Liz Thomas

Introduction

This chapter explores the implications for personal tutoring of greater student diversity and considers how first generation entrants and students from working class backgrounds could be better supported to succeed in higher education via an integrated and pro-active personal tutoring system. It begins by outlining some of the implications of widening participation within a mass system of higher education and explores the purpose of and alternative approaches to personal tutoring. Drawing on recent research with first generation entrants and working class students who withdrew from higher education, their difficulties are considered along with some of the ways in which effective personal tutoring could have supported them better and perhaps have prevented their leaving higher education. I conclude that personal tutoring potentially has an important role to play in supporting the widening of participation in mass HE but that many new students benefit from a proactive, integrated and structured approach to personal tutoring that enables them to regularly meet a member of staff on a one-to-one or small group basis so they can talk freely.

Widening participation in mass higher education

Widening participation has taken place in mass higher education; greater student diversity has been accompanied by an expansion in the numbers of students participating in HE. These co-tangent trends have resulted in an increased number of students from a wider range of backgrounds and worsening staff/student ratios. Expansion has not been accompanied by a comparable increase in unit resource (UUK, 2001), so there is greater reliance on large lectures and less small group teaching. Although widening participation has resulted in greater student diversity, students from lower socio-economic groups are still under-represented. This includes students from a wide range of educational and experiential backgrounds and students with access to less cultural capital (i.e. less family knowledge about higher education practices, norms and values etc). Widening participation and changes in student finance mean that the majority of students having an increased number of commitments beyond their education. For many of them, particularly those from low income groups, undertaking paid employment is a necessity (Susan and Williams, 2002), and often they work well in excess of the recommended number of hours (eg Sinclair and Dale, 2000; Noble, 2004). Greater diversity has resulted in more students with family responsibilities: to save money many young students live at home and study at a local institution – and may also be required to contribute to the family or community. These additional commitments, which have not traditionally encumbered students, reduce opportunities for participation in extra-curricular activities (Cooke *et al*, 2004; Blasko *et al*, 2003), or anything which is perceived to be non-essential, and this may include seeking additional support. Non-traditional students with these pressures often do not seek help as actively as their more traditional peers (Dodgson and Bolam, 2002; Thomas *et al*, 2002). Recent research found that many working class students had low levels of self-confidence and were hesitant to ask for academic and pastoral support when they needed it and that this contributed to a decision to withdraw from higher education early (Quinn *et al*, 2005).

Personal tutoring roles

Wheeler and Birtle (1993) describe the personal tutoring system as an 'anchor', which is a useful analogy incorporating images of a stable point of contact between the student and the institution, embedding students into the system and enabling them to remain in higher education and to complete their programme of study. In summary, personal tutoring can be seen to fulfil a number of roles for students: information about higher education processes, procedures and expectations; academic feedback and development; personal welfare support; referral to further information and support; a relationship with the institution and a sense of belonging. These are all crucial as students make the transition into higher education, which can be problematic for many students, especially those with little or no family experience of higher education (Quinn *et al*, 2005).

Information about higher education processes, procedures and expectations

Personal tutoring can provide information about higher education processes, procedures and expectations. For example, Forsyth and Furlong (2003) found that young people from non-traditional backgrounds had no prior knowledge of what student life involved. They were frequently unprepared for the amount of free time they had and were unsure of how to manage this productively. Participants in the UCAS (2002) study also felt they were underprepared for the transition from 'cosseted learning style to mass independent HE' (p30). Evidence of their lack of knowledge of the reality of student life was found in smaller studies at one post-1992 institution by Leathwood and O'Connell (2003) and Read *et al* (2003). Both studies found that non-traditional students including mature, first generation and ethnic minority students felt that they were expected to be too independent too early and were shocked by the lack of supervision and guidance. Personal tutoring can provide guidance and structure, especially in those early days.

Academic feedback and development

Anxiety about higher education arises because new students do not know what is expected from them academically. For example, they have concerns about how to study and learn (Quinn *et al*, 2005) and about undertaking assignments, knowing how to structure academic writing and examination standards (Murphy and Fleming, 2000). Learning transition and the learning and teaching environment are highly influential on students' success (Laing, and Robinson, 2003; Davies, 1999) and may contribute to students' decisions to leave higher education early (Quinn *et al*, 2005). Personal tutors can provide guidance about academic norms and practices and if they are engaged in teaching these students directly, they can also provide formative feedback to equip students with the information and skills they need to develop for academic success. According to Juwah *et al* (2004) good feedback has the following benefits:

- facilitates the development of self-assessment (reflection) in learning
- encourages teacher and peer dialogue around learning
- helps clarify what good performance is (goals, criteria, standards expected)
- provides opportunities to close the gap between current and desired performance
- delivers high quality information to students about their learning

- encourages positive motivational beliefs and self-esteem
- provides information to teachers that can be used to help shape teaching

Personal welfare support

Personal tutoring has traditionally had a welfare role, supporting students with personal difficulties. Indeed, in Owen's (2002) study, students perceived the primary role of personal tutors to be to solve students' problems, particularly for students living away from home. Students can experience difficulties in relation to family issues, illness, bereavement, childcare, part time employment, time management, stress and financial issues. Research suggests that mature students often struggle with many of these issues and that this may be the cause of their early withdrawal (Ozga and Sukhnandan, 1998), while working class students may be less willing to seek help (Quinn, 2004).

Referral to further information and support

Personal tutors can be viewed as a first point of contact for students who have difficulties or as a mechanism to pick up students who are struggling either personally or academically. Tutors are not normally expected to be able to cope with or solve these problems themselves: their role is to direct students to appropriate professional help such as that provided by Student Services (Thomas *et al*, 2002, p58 and Grant in this volume). However, students do not always feel it is appropriate to talk to personal tutors about these issues, especially if they are also their academic teachers who assess them.

Institutional relationship and sense of belonging

Many students from non-traditional and under-represented groups feel excluded or alienated by their higher education institution(Bamber and Tett, 2000; Read *et al*, 2003 and Thomas, 2002). For example, Read *et al.* (2003) found that students from non-traditional backgrounds are disadvantaged by an institutional culture that places them as 'other': the typical student is often assumed to be young, and with no other responsibilities – and this influences policies, practices and projections about HE. However, academic staff's attitudes are influential in assisting students to feel comfortable, or otherwise, within the institutional culture (Parker *et al*, 2005 and Thomas, 2002). Personal tutors can act as a bridge between students and the institution to help break down perceived barriers, and integrate them into the higher education community of staff and students. Tutoring in groups has the advantage of enabling students to engage with their peers and gain support from them – which is often an important source of help (Bamber and Tett, 2000, Thomas, 2002 and Hill in this volume).

Personal tutoring approaches and models

There is a wide range of personal tutoring systems in place in higher education institutions in the UK (Owen, 2002), many of which are being revised and developed to meet the changing needs of higher education in the 21st century (Yorke and Thomas, 2003, p70). Alternative approaches are underpinned by different philosophies or beliefs which inform how the system is structured. For example, personal tutoring can be provided for all students or just those in need of it; tutoring can be a proactive or reactive intervention; students can have restricted or easy access to staff; tutoring can be integrated into the curriculum, or provided as an additional support activity; tutor input can be structured or unstructured; and tutoring can be based on inter-personal relations or it can be professional and service-oriented. Earwaker (1992) identified three models of personal tutoring: a traditional 'pastoral' model; a model based on providing 'professional' support services and an integrated 'curriculum' model. It is useful to review these models in relation to the different informing principles outlined above, as this highlights how they differ from each other, and the potential strengths and weaknesses of each.

Pastoral model

In the pastoral (or traditional) model of personal tutoring, a specific member of staff is assigned to each student to provide personal and academic support. In these models all students are usually allocated a personal tutor (although this may not be true in every year of study), and thus tutors are nominally available for all students. In reality some students may make greater use of tutors than others, as personal tutoring provision is not integrated into the curriculum but is additional support that can be accessed by students as they deem fit, and some tutors may be perceived to be better than others (see Hixenbaugh *et al* in this volume). But as these systems rely on students arranging to see their tutors, they can be viewed to be reactive rather than proactive, and such a system is only operational when students have problems. Some students may fall through the net and not visit their tutor – perhaps because they lack confidence to seek help, or because the tutor is not available at a convenient time. Access to tutors is dependent on the availability of the tutor, which may be limited – for example research active staff may not spend much time on campus, or staff may have limited office hours, which do not coincide with when the student is available – this is particularly true for students who do not live in accommodation on or near the university and for those who have large part time work commitments. The pastoral model of personal tutoring does enable relations to develop between staff and students, but this is restricted to those who are able to make use of the provision. The type of support that students receive, however, is unstructured and may not meet the students' needs or expectations.

Owen's (2002) study revealed a revised approach to the traditional pastoral model – a pro-active and structured model. Each student is allocated a personal tutor, whom they are required to see at regular intervals throughout the year, irrespective of whether or not they are experiencing difficulties. More pro-active, structured approaches were also identified by Yorke and Thomas (2003), for example, one approach was to develop much tighter guidelines for students and staff about the purpose and contents of tutorials. In another institution tutorials were based around an agenda that had to be prepared in advance by the student. Owen (2002) argues that a more structured approach is necessary, which is less dependent upon 'the work schedule or goodwill of individual members of staff' (p20).

Professional models

Professional models of personal tutoring are centred around the provision of welfare and academic student services by professionally trained staff, who undertake this role on a full time basis. Such an approach means that support is always available for students in need, and that students can be sure of receiving a professional, structured approach which meets external quality standards. This, however, may mitigate against the development of staff/ student relations, as students are unlikely to see the same member of staff each time they use the service, as staff may be allocated on the basis of professional expertise, rather than because they know the student. This may therefore not contribute to integrating the student into the higher education institution. The professional system is predicated on student need, and could not hope to see all students, and it is therefore highly reactive, rather than proactive, and relies upon students identifying their problems and accessing support. Student services staff are aware that not all students who could benefit do use the support available, and reaching these students remains a challenge (Thomas *et al*, 2002). Student services is usually provided as additional support rather than in an integrated model and induction is used as a vehicle to inform students about what is available.

A number of hybrid professional models have developed, for example one-stop-shops and professional advisers based in academic departments. These approaches aim to overcome some of the shortcomings of the professional model outlined above. The one-stop-shop model of student services is increasingly popular (Layer *et al*, 2002); it aims to bring together a wide range of academic and pastoral support services in one place. This makes it easier for students to know where to go to find the support they need, and the inclusion of services such as the accommodation office (for students living in university-owned accommodation), the careers service, the finance office and health services, can remove the stigma of using student services and increase their availability to all students (i.e. students services are not just supporting students with problems). (See Thomas *et al*, 2002 for further details.)

Centralised student services, including one-stop-shops, can be too distant from students studying in their departments. This may be a geographical distance, especially in institutions that are not based on a single campus, or a perceived distance based on identity and sphere of influence. Professional advisers based in departments or faculties bring the support closer to home. They often have a brief to keep an eye on all students, perhaps by monitoring their attendance, and following up those who are persistently absent. Although such a service can rely on students accessing advisers, these are often proactive and follow up students who appear to be having difficulties. The support offered is more widely available (as it is a professional support post, rather than an academic post) and its contents is professional rather than personal. Nonetheless, students will see the same person, so relationships can be developed. This approach provides support that is additional to the core curriculum, but being based in the department may make it feel more connected that a centrally provided service.

Integrated curriculum model

The third model identified by Earwaker is the integrated curriculum model. Here, each student undertakes a module, with their personal tutor group, incorporating learning skills and information about the institution and higher education more generally. Earwaker identifies six objectives for support delivered via an integrated curriculum: to introduce students to the institution; to show them what is expected of them; to help them understand their own learning; to develop institutional and discipline expectations and engagement; to encourage and facilitate mutual peer support; and to enable students to seek professional help when required. Personal tutoring is time-tabled (and in some examples accredited), it is therefore required that students attend, and that staff teach the sessions. When support is integrated into the curriculum, especially when it is accredited, all students benefit from the provision, and not just when they are in need. This represents a proactive approach which allows relationships to develop between students and staff and peers.

Working class students' experiences in higher education

Recent research with young working class students who have withdrawn from their local post-1992 universities identified a wide range of reasons why students leave early (Quinn *et al*, 2005). The research was undertaken qualitatively and included one-to-one face-to-face and telephone interviews with 67 ex-students. Participants told their stories about leaving, which often involved the complex interplay of several factors. In this section brief summaries of two students' experiences are presented, and these are analysed to consider how personal tutoring might have enabled students to succeed in higher education.

Sarah's story

Sarah was the first person in her family to go to university. She attended college before going on to university and felt that college lecturers gave far more help and support to their students than did university lecturers. *'You don't want to bother the lecturer because we don't think they care...'* Sarah described the difficulties of sometimes not understanding lectures but not wanting to be the person to say so in front of the class.

Sarah expected university to be different to college but did not expect it to be so difficult to ask for help. She reflected that part of her difficulty lay in the fact that she had chosen the wrong path and if she could turn the clock back she would have chosen what her 'heart told her to do' rather than what she was advised. But once she was at university she was too scared to ask for the help she needed. *'Someone to listen to...is not a big thing to ask from a university'* and she suggested that students should be made aware that there is someone willing to listen to problems other than the lecturers. She felt that universities should be more aware that people are scared to come forward with problems:

They can cover their backs by saying we have got a notice-board that says there's a counsellor, but that's not the same as somebody coming into class and saying we are here if you need to speak to use and you can come in confidence – it is nothing to be ashamed of. 'You are just a number. I am a statistic of somebody that has dropped ...Nobody realised there was anything wrong and no-one asked...The doctor was the first person I spoke to about the problem and she was the only one that said 'I understand'...

Adapted from Quinn *et al*, 2005, pp 20-21

Sarah needed academic support, but she was too embarrassed to ask for clarification in lectures, and she didn't want to bother the lecturers afterwards. She thought she had chosen the wrong course, but did not feel that there was anyone there to listen to her – so the first person she spoke to was the doctor. A personal tutoring system that meant she had contact with a personal tutor as a matter of course could have provided her with a range of support to overcome these difficulties, and probably prevented her from leaving higher education unnecessarily. A personal tutor could have assisted Sarah to understand the differences between college and university, and provided her with the academic support she needed. Tutoring would have offered the opportunity to talk about her HE experience, either with the tutor or with peers, and she could have been given information about changing courses. She may also have been referred to additional support services if these were required.

Michael's story

Michael comes from a working-class background and is an only child. He didn't want to move too far away from his home town, so he applied to his local university to do an HND in computing.

I looked at the degree course and I thought it would be too difficult for me. ...When I first spoke to the university they told me the HND course was running, when I came to sign they announced that this course is no longer available. They then told me about this Computer Science course. I had only put one option on my UCAS, so then I panicked because I had everything set up for going. I had Halls to stay in. I panicked: everyone else was going. I didn't want to be left at home when everybody else was away... I just panicked and did the degree.

The class sizes were very big. There was no personal contact...I enjoy studying but there was no personal contact when I ran into problems with the course. It was very intimidating, sitting in a class of 150. The lecturer didn't even know you. If I had a problem it was difficult to get some help, then that problem would get worse and worse ... It would have been better if they'd taught us in small groups where we could sit down at the PC and show us what they meant instead of just talking and talking...There were times when I found it really hard to cope with.

Michael did seek help but was not offered any advice about changing course:

It was a case of, it is your course, you picked it, and you are in it....If I could have changed to another subject that had similar modules maybe I could have changed instead of dropping out and wasting the year, leaving with nothing.....I stayed until May... more or less to the exams. I realised that in no way was I fit to do them. The course was too much.

Michael is now doing a HND in Business IT at college.

Adapted from Quinn *et al,* 2005, pp 40-41

Michael started the course with academic concerns about the degree programme, rather than the HND he had originally applied to do. He struggled with the work and found the large group teaching further impeded his learning. He felt unable to seek help with his academic problems. When he did seek support he was not given advice about changing courses or claiming credit and was left with little option but to leave the university. A personal tutor could have provided initial reassurance about his academic ability, and/ or referred him for additional academic support; they could also have offered some feedback about his academic performance. Personal tutoring in a small group would have enabled Michael to have closer contact with a member of staff and maybe to have developed a relationship with them: this might have facilitated him to ask for academic help at an earlier point, and this might have relieved the need to change course/leave the institution; alternatively a tutor could have directed him to a more appropriate programme before it was necessary to leave and re-enter HE the following year.

Conclusion

Personal tutoring potentially has an important role to play in supporting widening participation in mass HE, as shown in these two stories, which are representative of the many students interviewed as part of this research project. There are alternative models of personal tutoring but they appear to favour different types of students. Warren (2002) draws on research from South Africa and Australia and defines three models of curriculum support: separate, semi-integrated or integrated. A separate approach implies that the intervention of support is offered in addition to mainstream teaching, as in the traditional pastoral model or professional model. A semi-integrated approach includes interventions which are closely aligned to the curriculum, which are developmental rather than remedial and appropriate to the subject domain. This may be more like having advisers at the departmental and faculty level to tailor support to complement the curriculum. Integrated approaches make the development central to the learning experience within the discipline context. Warren's analysis suggests that semi-integrated and integrated approaches are more effective than separate interventions.

Research with working class and first generation entrants suggests that these students are particularly likely to benefit from a proactive, integrated and structured approach that prioritises relationships, rather than the onus being on students to access services when they need them from staff they do not know. Similarly, Owen (2002) critiques the approaches she has identified and the models outlined by Earwaker (1992). She concludes that the curriculum model, based on providing integrated support through the modules offers great potential. The challenge that remains for many institutions is to decide how to develop a more integrated and proactive personal tutoring system, which is not overly onerous for staff, makes appropriate use of professional services, and is cost effective.

4

Rescuing the personal tutor:
Lessons in costs and benefits

Ormond Simpson

Introduction

Follow the money – Deep Throat

There are many excellent reasons for promoting the idea of personal tutoring in UK higher education. Some arguments centre around essentially ethical ideas of giving students a fair and just deal, some around the fact that as participation widens, increasing numbers of less well-prepared students enter higher education and require increased support. This chapter will attempt to argue the case for personal tutoring from a financial perspective – in the words of Bernstein and Woodward's secret source in the Watergate affair Deep Throat, it will try to 'Follow the money'.

This approach is important because senior university budget holders are more likely to be influenced by arguments that invoke financial logic. This is not to be cynical about university management: any budget holder faced with conflicting demands must consider carefully where investment is most effective: personal tutoring is an expensive activity. If there is an argument that personal tutoring not only makes practical sense but can be justified financially, it is more likely to attract senior management support. This chapter will attempt to show that personal tutoring not only makes sense financially to institutions and students but that there are circumstances in which it can even return a financial surplus to the institution.

The first step in following the money is to link personal tutoring with student retention.

Personal tutoring and student retention

Student retention is a complex affair in which there are many variables. Trying to separate out the effects of a personal tutoring system is very difficult. Perhaps the only way would be to undertake a medical trial in which two groups of students with similar characteristics were compared, one group receiving no personal tutoring, or a placebo – although it's difficult to imagine what form that might take – and the other receiving some kind of personal tutoring. Such a trial would hardly be ethical. Another way might be to introduce a personal tutoring scheme into a student support system as an innovation and see if this improved student performance. Such experiments would still be difficult given the many variables that contribute to student success. The Open University inadvertently set up the conditions for such a trial when it changed its student support systems around 1996, effectively abolishing its previous personal tutoring system.

The personal tutor in the Open University

When setting up the Open University (OU) in the late 1960s, its planning group recognised that that the many poorly qualified students entering the university would probably require high levels of support. They therefore designed a personal tutor system as part of its support programme. These personal tutors were called counsellors and their remit was to give non-academic support (Simpson, 2002) to students, helping them to adapt to distance learning and progress their studies. Counsellors were the equivalent of the personal tutor in conventional higher education.

In addition OU students were allocated a course tutor for their particular course who was responsible for teaching that course. When students moved onto their next course they were allocated another tutor but the counsellor remained responsible for their non-academic support (OU students may take six to twelve courses over four to eight years for their degree). Tutors and counsellors were both part time members of the OU's staff.

From the late 70s the roles of tutor and counsellor were amalgamated into a tutor-counsellor role, where the tutor appointed for a new student's first course was also their counsellor and remained so for the rest of the student's studies. This system was thought to work well; tutor-counsellors were able to make good relationships with their students whilst teaching them during their first year and those relationships often endured for the remainder of the student's career.

However there were few attempts to collect evidence of the value of the tutor-counsellor role. Simpson (1977) found that students overwhelmingly agreed with the statement that 'there should be a person in the OU system who has a personal knowledge of their progress and to whom students could refer.' But this finding could be criticised on grounds that it was difficult to challenge this statement and that no alternatives were offered. When change to the role was proposed there was therefore little objective evidence of its value.

The effective elimination of the personal tutor in the OU
Proposals for change arose because of changes in OU entry. Prior to 1992 nearly all students entered on the same range of courses – the OU's five Foundation courses – and tutor counsellors were therefore appointed to these courses. In the early 90s when the university started allowing students to enter on any one of its 150 courses the picture became more complex. There were two possible options for changing the counselling system:

- Students entering on non-foundation courses could be allocated a counsellor who wouldn't be their tutor. This was already the case for associate students studying one-off courses and it was clear that the relationship built up between counsellor and student was less satisfactory, given the lack of a teaching contact.
- All tutors could be designated tutor-counsellors. But apart from the increased payment costs involved it was thought that not all the OU's 5000 tutors would want to take on this role.

It was also believed that as the OU's programmes of study became more complex, it was unreasonable to expect part time staff to be able to answer the range of questions that students might ask. However, it was also clear that the counselling system was thought by senior management to be too expensive, although no figures were ever published.

So from 1996 the counselling role of the tutor-counsellor was gradually eliminated over several years and counselling was taken over by full time staff in the OU's thirteen regional centres on a reactive basis, with teams of three or four academic-related staff, supported by clerical staff servicing the needs of anything up to 15,000 students. Students still had a different course tutor for each course they studied and could refer to full time staff by phone, email and letter for non-academic support – essentially a call centre model of student support with no personal counselling.

The University recently invested a large sum, rumoured to be several million pounds, in a Customer Relation Management (CRM) system. This software maintains student records and allows the University to see what contacts the student has made with the University and what topics have been raised.

No effort was made to evaluate the effects on student learning at any stage in these changes. Such evaluations would have been difficult since the multivariate nature of the causes of student drop out is well-known (Woodley, 1987), but given the sums of money involved and the self-styled character of the university as a learning organisation it is surprising that no attempts were made to see if the modifications had been effective. Perhaps in the absence of any clear theory of student support, an institution's policies are likely to be influenced by the most powerful voices in the system.

Nevertheless there were dissenting voices to the changes, albeit from frontline staff. In general such staff are usually denied the knowledge – particularly the financial knowledge – to make cases against developments sponsored by senior management. And once senior management have backed a project then a version of the 'Titanic Effect' (Watt, 1974) may come into operation: no-one looks out for icebergs.

Eliminating the personal tutor – the consequences

Despite the lack of evaluation it may now be possible to draw some conclusions about the implications of the abolition of the personal counsellor:

- Student retention on course. Student retention rates in the UKOU have been drifting downwards for a number of years but the rate at which they were declining appeared to accelerate over the period at which the tutor-counsellor role was eliminated – from around 1996 onwards – see figure 1 which uses data from the OU's Technology courses as an example.

- Student re-registration. In 2003 nearly 30 per cent of new students completing their first year did not carry on to a second: the proportion of students carrying on after their first year has been dropping since the early nineties – see figure 2.

Once again there is a small but definite drop in re-registration rates from 1996 onwards, although admittedly small in comparison with the long term drop from 1990.

Thus in two measures of student retention there are small but clear drops after 1996. These cannot be related definitively to the abolition of the personal counsellor but there were no other significant changes in the university at that time so that possibility must at least be kept in view.

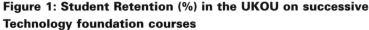

Figure 1: Student Retention (%) in the UKOU on successive Technology foundation courses

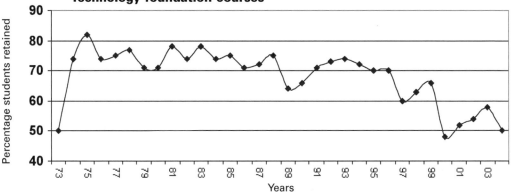

Percentage students retained

Years

Figure 2: Re-registration rates (%) of new students completing the previous year

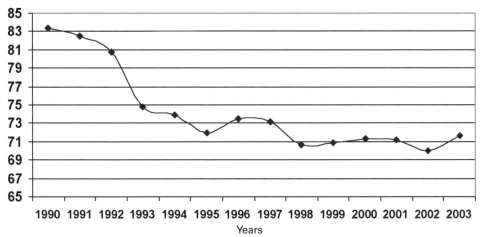

Percentage students re-registrating

Years

The personal tutor makes a come-back

Considerations like these led to attempts by junior staff to evaluate the effect of re-introducing the personal tutor in some way in small scale projects. One of the first to report was Simpson (2004). Around 3000 new students were identified as being particularly vulnerable to drop out by a statistical analysis of their entry characteristics. Half were proactively phoned before their courses started by a 'study adviser'. The call was relatively short (an average of 10 minutes) and its content was aimed at making a relationship with the student and enhancing both their integration with the institution and their motivation, using findings from the relatively recent field of positive psychology (Snyder *et al*, 2001). The other half, with the same levels of vulnerability, was kept as a control group. The experiment was repeated in three successive years (see Table 1).

On average the experimental group had a retention rate around 5 per cent higher then the control group. This may not sound like a large increase in retention. But students admitted to the OU are likely to be older than conventional students, to have lower qualifications on entry, to be in work and have family commitments. They are therefore more likely to experience institutionally unavoidable drop out due to illness, job changes and family commitments. It has been estimated that a 5 per cent increase in retention is nearly a third of the maximum possible increase in retention that is possible through institutional activities, although this estimate is open to question (Simpson, 2003).

It may strain credulity to suggest that this effect was due to one phone call. But the effects are clear and appear to be continuing. There are reasons why such a simple contact could have had such an effect:

- Student drop out in the OU is heavily front-loaded. About 15 per cent of students drop out before the course starts and another 30 per cent before submitting the first assignment. They have had little contact with their tutor and any teaching activity. Thus to effect retention an activity is likely to be focused before or at the start of the course, as this one was.
- There is no personal proactive contact from the university before courses start. Potential students are encouraged to enrol with the university on the Web and are unlikely to have any personal contact with the university before the course materials arrive. Thus a personal interactive contact would stand out and might have a marked result.
- The style of the contact was an individually-focused activity aimed at enhancing the student's motivation, rather than on identifying weaknesses. A contact based to some extent on evidence derived from an appropriate evidential basis in psychology has more effect than contacts without such a basis.

Costs and benefits of the OU study adviser activity to the institution

Since this exercise was carried out in isolation with balanced control groups, it is not unreasonable to infer a direct causal effect between the contact and the retention increase. It is then possible to isolate the costs and, to a lesser extent, the financial benefit of the contact and to calculate its return on investment. This can be done as follows:

Consider an activity applied to N students which costs £P per student and produces an increase in retention of r per cent. The total cost of the activity

Table 1 Differences in pass rates of contacted and non-contacted students 2002-2004

Year	Contacted group total	Contacted group withdrawn during course	% of contacted group withdrawn	Control group total	Control group with drawn during course	% of control group withdrawn	Difference in withdrawal rates contacted – control
2002	1433	272	18.98	1433	328	22.89	3.91
2003	1152	184	15.97	204	43	21.08	5.11
2004	910	158	17.36	97	21	21.64	4.28
Totals	**3495**	**614**	**17.57**	**1734**	**392**	**22.61**	**5.04**

will be £NP and the number of extra students retained will be Nr/100. The cost per student retained is then £NP/(Nr/100), which equals 100P/r.

In the OU exercise the increase in retention was around 5 per cent. The cost of the individual contact was estimated to be about £10 in staff time and over-heads (average call length was around 10 minutes and staff made about three calls an hour, the remainder of the time being used for recording and administration). Thus the cost per student retained was 100x10/5 = £200.

At first sight this figure is intimidating. It is hard to imagine a university budget holder allowing such expenditure, especially if applied to all new students. In the OU, with 35,000 new students a year, the overall expenditure would be £35,000x10 = £350,000 for an increase in retention of 35,000x5/100 = 1650 students, which does not sound like a bargain.

But as well as costs it is important to estimate benefits. In common with other UK universities the OU receives a grant from the Higher Education Funding Council for England, which is based on the number of students who complete their courses: the funding regime is more complex than this statement implies but it is sufficiently accurate for this analysis. This sum is currently about £1100 for a student completing a 60 credit point course. In addition there may be savings on recruitment costs. If drop out is reduced fewer students need to be recruited to maintain steady numbers. Currently it costs the OU around £500 in marketing costs per new student recruited. If it assumed that a proportion of that – say £200 – might be saved through increased retention, the total income to the OU for every student retained rises to around £1300.

Thus the surplus income for every student retained is £(1300 – 200) = £1100 which is a return on investment of 1100/200 = 550 per cent. Were the activity applied to all new students and a similar level of retention achieved for a similar cost, the total surplus income to the university would be £1650x1100 = £1.8m. Clearly this figure is approximate but nevertheless it shows that it is possible to increase retention at least at zero cost and possibly even to make some small surplus.

The attraction of not only increasing student retention but possibly making a surplus was the point at which OU senior university management started to take notice and consequently this activity is being mainstreamed throughout the university from 2005 on. Clearly further proactive contact beyond the initial call might increase retention further and some limited work is being undertaken to investigate this possibility. But more contacts may eventually produce an effect of diminishing returns: Case and Elliot (1997) suggest, from an evaluation of an online programme in the US, that the optimum number of contacts is five. But how far this finding is reliable or applicable to conventional UK higher education remains to be seen.

As well as mainstreaming this activity, the OU is going to try to use the same adviser to make the proactive contact with the same student each time. The step after that will obviously be to make the study adviser reactively contactable by the student. If and when those characteristics are established, the OU will have in effect have reintroduced its personal tutor system some years after it was formally abolished.

It is unwise to draw substantial conclusions about personal tutoring in UK universities from one activity in a non-typical university such as the OU. There is clearly a big difference between a system that is based on one proactive phone call and a full personal tutor system. Nevertheless, there is an implication, to put it no more strongly, that as Chapman (2003) says 'to increase retention you must personalise your relationship with your students' and that an increase in retention can go a long way to funding such personalisation.

Costs and benefits of personal tutoring to students

Clearly it is not only the institution which has a financial interest in student retention. From 2006 students will be investing substantially larger sums in their education through increased fees as well as (in full time education) suffering loss of earnings over the study period. It is notoriously difficult to estimate the return on that investment but various authorities have attempted to assess the graduate premium: the extra amount a graduate could hope to earn over a lifetime, compared with a non-graduate. Figures from Walker and Zhu (2003) suggest a graduate premium of £200,000. If the Return on Investment (RoI) to students is defined as the graduate premium divided by their initial investment, that RoI is around 600 per cent. It is widely thought that this RoI must decrease with higher levels of participation in higher education, but evidence (Simpson, 2006) from countries such as Sweden and Australia, which already have higher levels, suggest that the RoI is holding up reasonably steadily. In the OU the RoI for student investment appears to be higher than for conventional universities at around 2200 per cent. This is mostly due to the absence of the loss of earnings factor, although lower fees also have an effect.

No discussion of any investment is complete without an evaluation of the risk attached to that investment; in universities that is the risk of drop out. We cannot be sure that a student's investment is entirely lost when they drop out but it seems probable. If so then that risk is high by standard financial criteria; on average in higher education it is around 20 per cent; in the OU it is nearly 50 per cent. In fact the risk to a student's investment in higher education is currently greater than putting their money into wildcat oil well drilling (Simpson, 2006 *op cit*).

Given that high risk to a student's investment, it may be that students will want greater guarantees of returns on their investment by choosing institutions where that risk is lower – institutions with lower rates of drop out. Thus the pressure for institutions to develop retention-friendly policies may increase and students and parents may demand higher levels of support to protect their investment. The most obvious form of support is likely to be through the development of a personal tutor system.

Implications of the cost-benefit analysis for personal tutoring systems in conventional universities

The findings from the OU experiment might suggest ways forward for university staff attempting to develop personal tutor strategies in their institutions:

■ do the research to link proactive support to student retention for the proposed system. That should include an international literature survey. For example there is evidence from distance education literature of the retention effects of proactive contact, such as Rekkedahl, Visser, and Chyung, all quoted in Simpson (2003). Some findings are also costed – Mager (2003) in the University of Ohio found an increase in retention of 4 per cent with a return of investment of 660 per cent

■ with the help of university statisticians, develop methods of identifying your most vulnerable students so that proactive contact resources can be targeted on them

■ attempt to undertake a cost-benefit analysis for the personal tutor strategy – it may be possible to enlist the help of the university's finance division (universities have a wealth of internal expertise at their disposal which is not always applied to their own concerns)

■ make the case to university senior management for increased funding for the personal tutor system, based on this analysis

■ develop a model of personal tutoring which is soundly based in psychology (again universities may already have the expertise), which addresses student retention. The key may lie in using proactive inter-active contacts with individuals which are based on the findings of posi-tive psychology (Snyder and Shane, 2001).

Much has been written recently about the concept of the 'student as cus-tomer'. But this may already be outdated and about to be replaced by the con-cept of the student as investor – and one who will increasingly be looking for a reasonable return on their investment. If this is the case, the introduction, development or rescuing of personal tutor systems becomes a matter of urgency. In future all higher education institutions will need to follow the money.

5

Student perspectives on personal tutoring: What do students want?

Paula Hixenbaugh, Carol Pearson and David Williams

Introduction

Academic institutions are facing new challenges in the context of government policy for the continued expansion of higher education and the focus on increasing the participation of those groups previously underrepresented. It is not enough to widen participation without also ensuring that the necessary structures are in place to maximise the chances of students completing their degrees. Increasingly, student support is being recognised as an important element in student success. Personal tutoring can play a key role in enabling students to integrate into the social and academic systems of university. This chapter reports on a review of the personal tutoring system at the Regent Campus, University of Westminster. It focuses on what students want and need from a personal tutoring system. Recommendations are made for enhancing personal tutoring systems to improve the quality of the relationship between students, staff and institutions.

Context

In the context of the widening participation agenda, the current literature suggests, and indeed government officials are explicit about the emphasis on a student-centred approach. A number of institutions across the sector have identified that student support is a key element in retaining students. In their review of student retention in the North East of England, Dodgson and Bolam (2002) found that although the region's universities provide an extensive range of student support services, the majority of students in their survey used only two – the student's union and the personal tutor. There were high rates of use of the personal tutoring system, however, 'the extent to which students found this useful varied quite a lot, implying its usefulness is dependent upon the problem and the relationship with the tutor' (p44). In 2005 the Student Retention Team at the University of Teesside identified that 'a key factor in student success appears to be the quality of support they receive from staff and the extent to which staff and students communicate effectively with each other.' (p23).

In its report on *Improving Student Achievement in English Higher Education*, the National Audit Office (2002) found that although all of the institutions of higher education allocate students to personal tutors, the approach to pastoral care varies widely both between and within institutions. They found that 'much of the responsibility for identifying and addressing academic or learning support needs rests with the personal tutor' (p29). However, there is little research on what students actually want from a personal tutoring system. At the University of Westminster we surveyed first year students and personal tutors in the spring of 2003 about their opinions of the strengths and weaknesses of the personal tutoring system.

The University of Westminster

Founded in 1838 as Britain's first polytechnic, the University currently has more than 23,800 students, of whom 75 per cent are undergraduates. It has a long history of providing education to non-traditional student populations, and is justly proud of the diversity of its student mix. The latest HESA return (2005) indicates that 42.8 per cent of students are White, 11.2 per cent Black, 23 per cent Asian, 5.1 per cent Chinese and other, 3.0 per cent mixed, and 15 per cent refused information. In terms of gender, the undergraduate population has more female students (56%). Ninety six per cent of the full time first degree student population come from state schools or colleges and 43 per cent are from NS-SEC classes 4,5,6, and 7. These figures are significantly above the locally adjusted institutional benchmarks published by HEFCE of 91 per cent and 36 per cent respectively. The proportion of new entrants to full time degree study who were mature (over 21) was 30 per cent in 2003/04 (latest HESA performance indicator data). More than 4,000 international students, from over 150 countries, make Westminster one of the top fifteen most popular UK universities for international students. Approximately 700 teaching staff are supported by up to 1,000 visiting lecturers. The University has four discipline-specific campuses – three in London's West End and one at Harrow.

The following review of personal tutoring was carried out on undergraduate courses at the Regent Campus, in the West End of London. The campus consists of two major schools, the Law School, and the School of Social Science, Humanities and Languages. In the latest HESA return (2005) there were 2,519 students on undergraduate courses, approximately 735 of them in their first year.

Undergraduate Tutoring Policy

The University has recently completed a review of the personal tutoring system and will implement a new tutoring policy in the 2006/07 academic year. However, the current University policy document contains the following policy regarding personal tutoring:

1. The tutorial and student support system combines the roles of personal tutor and academic tutor to provide advice and guidance to students throughout their course. Minimally, a two-tier system is adopted uniformly across the institution to meet students' needs in terms of advice on the educational coherence of their chosen study programmes and to provide basic pastoral care. Students must have access to a designated Personal Tutor and School/Campus Senior Tutors.

2. Each School must designate Personal Tutors. Each student must have access to a specific Personal Tutor who may remain their individual tutor throughout the whole period of study. As far as possible, students should be designated Personal Tutors who are involved in the delivery of their course.

3. The responsibilities of Personal Tutors are as follows:

    (i)   To be the first point of contact of tutees, providing associated pastoral care, advice and support to assist them in developing fully their academic potential

    (ii) To monitor the academic performance of their tutees and keep Course/ Programme Leaders informed

    (iii) To identify tutees with particular educational support needs and advise on appropriate procedures

    (iv) To refer tutees for more specialised pastoral guidance as appropriate to School/Campus Senior Tutors and/or Services for Students

    Responsibilities (v) – (xi) can be allocated either to the Personal Tutor, or, if more appropriate, to (an)other member(s) of staff such as Course Leader, Year Leader or Route Co-ordinator (as determined by the Head of School):

    (v)   To assist students through induction procedures

    (vi) To advise students on the educational coherence of their choice of modules and the implications for their future studies

    (vii) To advise students on time management in order to assist them in meeting coursework deadlines

    (viii) To advise students on assessment procedures and structures

(ix) To inform students about credit accumulation

(x) To draw the attention of students to the University's Assessment Regulations

(xi) To draw the attention of students to the requirements of professional bodies where relevant

It is assumed that subject specific advice on modules will be provided to students by Module Leaders or the member of staff responsible for delivering the module.

4. Each Head of School must appoint an Interdisciplinary Studies Personal Tutor to provide (or co-ordinate if numbers are too large) tutorial support as described in this policy for IDS students based in the School.

5. The number of Personal Tutors in each School is to be determined by the total number of undergraduate students for which the School has academic responsibility and a maximum number of 30 students per Personal Tutor is recommended.

Review of the Personal Tutoring System

The following are selected issues arising from the review of personal tutoring in Regent Campus, undertaken with the support of a small successful bid for Widening Participation funding. It was recognised through other reviews at the University that the first year or semester was a critical time for students' adjustment to University. Therefore, this review targeted the experiences of first year students and the tutors who worked with them. The review included:

■ A questionnaire to all teaching staff sent by email

■ A questionnaire to first year students across the campus, distributed in first year core modules

■ A series of interviews with first year course representatives from Psychology, Modern Languages, English, and Law

■ Follow-up focus groups with 48 first year psychology undergraduates and 15 personal interviews with first, second and third year psychology undergraduates

The following are highlights from each area of the review.

Staff Questionnaire

Thirty eight personal tutors (of a possible 86) returned completed questionnaires. They were distributed across the variety of courses in the campus.

Tutors who thought that the number of tutees they oversaw was about right numbered 52.6 per cent; 34.2 per cent thought they had too many, while 7.9 per cent thought they could have more. It is interesting that there was no relationship between the number of tutees reported by the tutor and their assessment of whether or not this was a reasonable number.

However, there was agreement that first year students have the greatest need for personal tutoring. The majority considered that the current personal tutoring system was working well for both staff and students (62.6%).

Student Questionnaire

The student questionnaire included demographic information, such as gender, age *etcetra* and how often they had seen their tutor, whether they had considered dropping out of University and if so, who they talked to about this. Likert style questions (from 1=not at all to 5=a lot) explored the students' experience of the personal tutoring system in terms of how often they saw their tutor, how important it was to have the same tutor throughout their course, whether or not the tutor was accessible, how much they needed to see their tutor, how satisfied they were with the personal tutoring system, and how helpful the personal tutor had been in a variety of areas. Two open-ended questions asked students what they thought the personal tutoring system should provide and how it could be improved.

Questionnaires were returned by 281 students (38%) (226 female, 55 male).

Of the respondents, only 36.1 per cent were the first person in their family to attend university. Most students (69.8%) met their personal tutor during induction week but only 89.5 per cent of students knew who was their personal tutor.

The majority of students reported not needing to see their personal tutor (55%), although a small proportion had seen their personal tutor on fifteen or more occasions. The data suggest that students wanted to see their personal tutor more often than they needed to see them. It may be that students gain a sense of support from the knowledge that they can approach their personal tutor, regardless of whether or not they need to.

Nearly 19 per cent of students indicated that they had considered dropping out of university but had decided to stay. Financial difficulty was a prominent reason for potential withdrawal (16.3%). Volume, pressure and difficulty of work was the next most prominent (14.3%), followed by feeling overwhelmed (10.2%). It is reasonable to consider that the last two categories could be made into one: an overall lack of confidence in their ability to cope with the demands of university. The major source of support/advice about withdrawing from the course was the student's own social support network. This is in line with expectations but it is cause for concern that 26.3 per cent of students did not discuss their concern with anyone and only two of the 38 students who responded to this question mentioned their personal tutor.

The majority of students believed that the personal tutoring system should provide advice and support, both academic and personal (figure 1 below). Most students also thought that it was important to have the same personal tutor throughout their course. Overall, students considered that tutors are accessible during office hours but wanted more office hours and greater accessibility.

Figure 1. What do you think the personal tutoring system should provide?

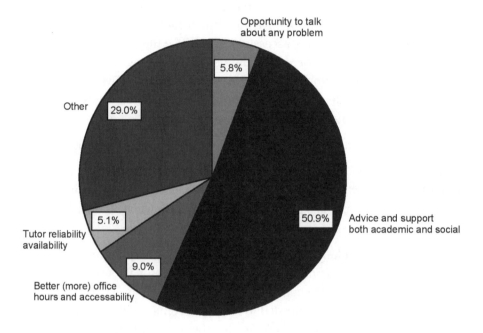

Answers to the question, 'How satisfied are you with the personal tutoring system?', were distributed more or less along a normal curve from '1 = not at all' to '5 = a lot' with 3 ('somewhat') the most frequent response.

In response to the open-ended questions, some students were extremely happy with their personal tutors, while a small number expressed dissatisfaction. Of those who were dissatisfied, students expressed the feeling that tutors needed to understand students better, be more prepared to cooperate with them, be reliable and form closer links with them. When asked how the personal tutoring system could be improved (see figure 3, page 52), the majority of students wanted structured, regular sessions that included active feedback (to know how I'm doing). A number of respondents suggested that these meetings should be compulsory.

Figure 2. How satisfied are you with the personal tutoring system?

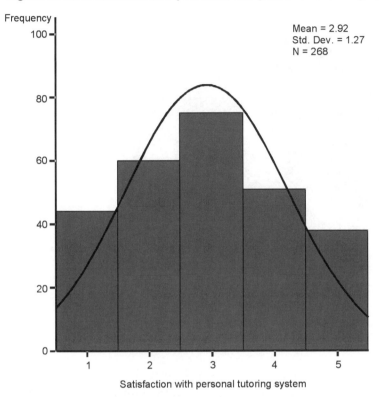

Satisfaction with personal tutoring system

To summarise, the data from the questionnaire supported the conclusion that although the personal tutorial system was working well in places, a number of students wanted the system to be more structured and active.

Student Interviews

To gain further insight into the personal tutoring system, four interviews were undertaken, using a semi-structured interview protocol. The protocol was developed to ascertain students' views on their first contact with their personal tutor, their personal experience of, and the factors important to, personal tutoring, as well as suggestions for changes to the system. In addition to the original research, four further focus group interviews were undertaken the following academic year with first year psychology undergraduates and individual interviews were conducted with 15 first, second and third year psychology undergraduates, in which questions pertaining to the personal tutoring system were included. An academic member of staff undertook the original focus group interviews but was only known to one of the interviewees. Two independent interviewers, to ensure complete confidentiality

Figure 3. How could the personal tutoring system could be improved?

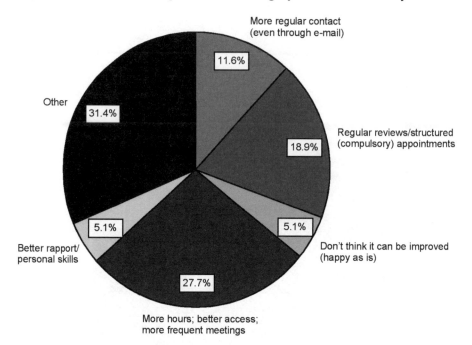

and to give students the opportunity to speak freely about their experiences, undertook all the additional focus groups and individual interviews. A thematic analysis, using grounded theory principles, was undertaken on the data.

Eight first year undergraduate students, who had been elected as course representatives from four degrees across the university, volunteered to take part in the original study; these included Psychology, Modern Languages, English and Law. A further 48 first year psychology undergraduates participated in four additional focus groups and 15 first, second and third year psychology undergraduates participated in individual interviews.

Results
First contact experience
Students' first contact experiences with their personal tutors were positive: all students reported that they had met their personal tutors as part of their induction week programme. In all cases the initial meeting involved an exchange of relevant information, including contact details. Some students indicated that extra reinforcement of issues such as the role of module and course leaders, as well as what seminars and lectures entail, would also be

useful at this stage. All but one student reported being happy with this initial contact:

> I met my own personal tutor the day we came for induction, we were given our personal tutors because we have a group. We had a group discussion and she gave us the telephone number for her, just gave us all the necessary information we needed.

Personal experience of tutoring system
Amount of contact

Students reported having infrequent contact with their personal tutors after the initial induction contact, although reassuringly all first year students had seen their personal tutors at least twice, some far more, during the academic year. Interestingly, second and third year students suggested that frequent contact had become less of an important issue for them but what was more important was knowing that it was available to them if they needed it.

> It's decreased because for one thing I have no time but because I have more friends now but I know I can go to her when I really need to.

Accessibility

This was a major issue raised by all students which they believed to be important to many of their fellow students. Students considered the issue of accessibility on two different levels, both the practical and personal level.

Practical Level – all students, bar one, reported that their personal tutors were accessible during office hours, by email or telephone, although all stressed the importance of speedy replies to emails and phone messages.

> It's quite easy actually, although his office hours are only 4-5 on a Tuesday, it was quite easy just to go and see him as well. If you emailed him, straight-away he'd get back to you within a couple of hours and he'd make it easy enough to access his area, and come and see him in his office. So yes, he's always been accessible.

Personal Level – all students, apart from one, who had a very positive experience, reported that on a personal level their personal tutor was perceived as being less accessible. There was some indication that students saw the personal tutors as 'busy people' which made them reluctant to 'bother them'. The issue of gender was also raised, although it appeared to be a general issue that female staff were more approachable than male staff. Indeed approachability was an important issue for all students. This seemed to be related to personal tutors 'general manner' and 'tone of voice'. For some students the age difference between themselves and their tutor created barriers. Familiarity was also viewed as a problem by most of the students because limited contact meant less familiarity with their tutor. However, on a more positive note, others found their personal tutor to be approachable because they were 'sociable, helpful, and understanding'. Indeed, some students suggested that the overall problem was with student expectations. Students felt that their behaviour and attitudes towards tutors were based on the constant attention they had received from tutors and teachers at school or college. At university it was simply a matter of role reversal, in that it was up to students to make the first move. Having done so, students found that tutors were more approachable than they had first thought.

> It took me a while to realise that you had to go to them, they weren't going to come to you all the time like at school but when you do they are really helpful. I didn't realise at first.

Support
The issue of support was raised by all students and was split into two main areas, personal and academic support. All the students felt that their own experiences reflected those of their fellow students.

Personal Support – none of the students reported having seen their tutors about personal matters. Only one student felt that this would have been appropriate had personal issues arisen – the others felt unable to go to their tutor with personal problems, despite the fact that they had experienced difficulties during the year.

> I don't really feel that I can go to her for personal issues, I don't feel comfortable with her in that role. I just don't want to really talk to her about them .... I go to my friends instead.

Academic Support – in complete contrast to personal support, all students throughout their first year, and in subsequent years, had sought academic support. All students, except one, reported being happy with the academic support they had received. Academic support seemed to take two forms: *University Processes* advice was given on processes such as *plagiarism* and *internal referrals* ie fees and module enquires; *Course Related Issues* advice in terms of referrals to appropriate material ie websites and other staff, although the issue of whether all tutors had the same level of knowledge was thought to pose problems for some of them.

> I've just been lucky I guess – I know other students who haven't been able to get as much help as I have.

Suggestions for change

Students made six main suggestions to improve the personal tutoring system:

Enforced meetings – all students felt that meetings with personal tutors were important throughout the first year. Although drop-in sessions during office hours were seen to serve a purpose, it was felt that many students were reluctant to use the drop-in system. All of the students interviewed felt that enforced meetings throughout the year would be useful, suggesting that these should be both individual and group meetings, as well as there being timetabled or appointment-based sessions

Email contact – students should be made to contact their personal tutor on a regular basis by email

Academic tutorials – all students thought that it would be invaluable to have academic tutorials with their personal tutor in their first year: this would allow them to build group relationships, develop more familiarity with their tutor and allow time to discuss issues relating to the course

Selection of tutors – all students felt that in the light of their own, and fellow students experiences, that the university should be more selective about which staff are personal tutors to first year students

Mobile phones – perhaps indicative of the times, some students suggested that personal tutors should be able to contact students via mobile phones as these generally were the main contact source for students, especially those not living at home. In addition, some felt that tutors should have access to mobile phones so that contact could be made via text messaging

Coverage for absenteeism – there should be coverage for personal tutors who are absent for over one week.

In sum, there was evidence of good practice on the part of personal tutors. However, there was a general feeling that the tutoring system as it stands may be failing some students, particularly in terms of those experiencing personal difficulties. Some of the issues raised by students shed light on ways in which personal tutoring systems could be altered to address the problems experienced by first year students.

Conclusion

It is becoming clear that relationships are at the heart of the issue of the students' experience of university. Personal tutoring has a key role to play in providing this relationship. Our research indicates that students were reluctant to bring personal problems to their tutor; indeed none of those interviewed did so. Personal tutors were seen as busy people and students reported being reluctant to bother them. Students were unanimous in wanting scheduled meetings with their personal tutor and in feeling that these should occur throughout the first year.

In a climate of limited resources it is often difficult to provide the amount of staff contact time that students want. An e-mentoring scheme, developed in the Psychology Department at the University, pairs first year students with trained third year student mentors by email. The success of this scheme over the last four years (see Hixenbaugh *et al*, 2005) demonstrates that it is a cost effective and useful adjunct to the personal tutorial system.

The evidence clearly indicates that students want the personal tutoring system to provide regular and frequent scheduled meetings in which they are actively provided with feedback concerning their general progress. These students want personal tutors to take an active role throughout their degree and to be accessible, approachable and reliable. They want personal tutors who can relate to them, who are enthusiastic and care about them. It is recommended that universities devise personal tutoring structures that enable students and personal tutors to develop a relationship from the beginning of the students' entry to university. These meetings, group as well as individual, need to be scheduled and lack of attendance should be followed up.

Subsequent to the research reported here, the University of Westminster has undertaken a review of the personal tutorial system across the institution. As stated in the first paragraph of the new policy, the University has recognised that 'personal tutoring is fundamental in ensuring students are supported throughout their studies and are integrated into the University at an early stage.' A new tutoring policy has been developed and additional funds have been made available for implementation in the academic year 2006-2007. The focus of the new system is on more structured support in the first semester of the first year.

Section 2:
Institutional models and approaches

6

Enhancing the first year experience through personal tutoring

Heather Hartwell and
Crispin Farbrother

Introduction

The increasing diversity of the student population and pressure for less traditional class contact *inter alia* have led to the need to address student progression and retention issues in almost every UK higher education institution. Pastoral care and tutoring have been identified as approaches which may be successful in supporting and enhancing the first year for students in their new environment (Williamson, 2004). Previous research has identified that among first year students there is a general feeling of the need for security and to know 'how you are doing', to have a psychological 'stroking' (Hartwell and Farbrother, 2005). Personal tutor time could provide the forum for this type of individual contact and enable enhanced student support. However, a robust evaluation is required from both a student and staff perspective to facilitate evidence-based practice.

There is no consistent model of tutoring which operates throughout our institution and therefore it was initially decided to pilot an informal personal tutor scheme across the hospitality programmes within The School of Services Management. The project aimed to evaluate the contribution that personal tutors bring to supporting and enhancing the first year experience of students. The research methodology used focus groups conducted amongst students and semi-structured interviews with staff involved as pilot personal tutors. As a result a more structured approach was introduced which included a web-based resource called 'Stepping Stones'. This was intended to target ambition before arrival and aimed to encourage a culture of learning, together with a sense of community, while providing support pre-induction. A formalised curriculum model of personalised tutoring was also established. The mode of delivery encompassed five sessions which were structured, embedded in a first year unit (therefore counted as hours) and followed the set framework of:

- cultural/administration
- personal
- academic
- employment/real working environment
- career/placement

This too was evaluated and is the focus of this chapter.

Context

Historically akin to many HE institutions, personal tutors have not been appointed for courses in The School of Services Management at Bourne-mouth University. However, increasingly a wide variety of students from diverse academic backgrounds, (entry UCAS points range from 120 to 300+) have been accepted in a range of hospitality management programmes. The students follow a shared common curriculum in the first year and it has been recognised that a framework of personal tutoring could provide regular opportunities for feedback on assignments and action planning in relation to academic progress, as well as providing assistance to students in need. It is accepted that the majority of students will progress with only minimal requirement for personal tutor input. However, there are times when the pressures, whether academic or personal, can be so overwhelming that they impede effective functioning (University of Bath, http://internal.bath.ac.uk/tutors/).

The hospitality programmes recruit approximately ninety students per year into year one (level C) but unfortunately student retention is below both the school average and the university average: this has been so for a number of years. In the academic year 2003/2004 wastage for first years peaked at 40 per cent. It was felt that, in pursuance of the higher education strategy (HEFCE, 2003) for learning and teaching quality enhancement and to ascertain factors augmenting the first year experience, including retention, a preliminary study needed to be conducted to evaluate the first year learning environment (Hartwell and Farbrother, 2004). Conclusions reached were that to enhance the learning context first year hospitality students would like:

- small groups
- mixed ability
- support with the new environment of higher education
- peer assisted learning
- practical sessions

The concluding point led to further research (Hartwell and Farbrother, 2005) being developed in the area of first year student support. Two key issues identified were that students have a 'need for security' and would like some form of formal or informal progress report during the academic year. The second key area identified was the intangible notion of psychological stroking. The research showed that there was no commentary on students' formative learning and development. The study also allowed some reflection on when to start the support mechanisms required by first year students.

Present Culture

The School of Services Management has a culture of open door support for students: all staff display their weekly schedules on their doors and students can Stop and Knock when the tutor is in or book whenever there is space available on the timetable. Feedback from students constantly show this as a strength, although it is time-consuming for staff. The demands are often curriculum-based; however, pastoral concerns are also addressed. In addition to the open door culture there is also a formal process whereby students can go to their year tutor or to the hospitality programmes manager.

Support for students is also available through the Peer Assisted Learning (PAL) scheme developed from an early Fund for the Development of Teaching and Learning (FDTL) project, that has now been running for four years across the hospitality programmes. This places second year students with a first year group in a timetabled slot to facilitate learning skills and acclimatisation to higher education. Recently, a personal development website (PDP) (http://pdp.bournemouth.ac.uk) has been designed which engages students with the notion and skills of reflection in all aspects of their pedagogical and personal life. So that we could address the identified needs expressed by first year students and to demonstrate the institution's duty of care to exercise reasonable responsibility to attend to students' health and welfare, it was considered a good idea to trial a personal tutor system within the hospitality programmes. A robust evaluation from both student and staff perspectives would facilitate evidence based practice and inform future policy.

Intervention

Initially a scheme was put in place matching motivated first year tutors with eight tutees. This was then evaluated and extended to the current personal tutor structure which is run today. The present model is based on two approaches: first to target ambition prior to arrival (Stepping Stones) and secondly for a first year tutor to be responsible for both the welfare and academic guidance of a first year seminar group. With growing diversity and widening participation a robust support system is increasingly required. Students are entitled to a structure which ensures that they are 'known, tracked and supported' throughout their university careers (Owen, 2002). This can be achieved by a form of personalised tutoring. Research and our own experience indicates a preference for the curriculum model (Owen, 2002), as every student would take the course and first year tutors would be involved. Sessions would be timetabled and structured, ensuring consistency of contact. It has been demonstrated that with this approach better relationships develop between staff and students and among the peer group itself (Owen, 2002).

Stepping Stones to Higher Education

Stepping Stones is a novel web-based resource (http://sim/steps/index.html) that students are encouraged to access as soon as they accept their place at Bournemouth University. It provides activities/reading to be completed prior to induction and it presents information about studying at university that the student can assimilate in their own space and in their own time. Prospective students immediately become part of the community and one of the aims is to remove any trepidation they might have before the start of the academic year. Stepping Stones also includes an online self profiling questionnaire, which asks the student to reflect on their previous experiences of education and their expectations about coming to Bournemouth. This tool provides a unique opportunity for the students to become involved and engaged with their course before induction. Analysis of the questionnaires allows tutors to identify any students who may be vulnerable or at risk of leaving prematurely. Appropriate strategies can then be implemented at an early stage.

Stepping Stones is about boosting confidence, reducing anxiety and building relationships. The web pages contain, amongst other information, photographs of relevant staff and frequently-asked questions about accommodation and issues of a personal nature, together with testimonials from past students.

Personal Tutors

The curriculum model in practice means that each seminar group of approximately sixteen to eighteen students has a personal tutor. Each tutor is a member of the first year teaching team. There is much discussion about whether all staff should be personal tutors, so sharing the burden, or if targeted individuals, who are motivated, are a better choice. We have gone for the latter. These tutors will nurture and take students through induction week and thereafter meet the group of students once every five weeks, as the timetable operates on a five week rotation. These sessions will be structured, embedded in a first year unit (and therefore count as hours) and follow the set framework of:

- cultural/administration
- personal
- academic
- employment/real working environment
- career/placement

These sessions are discussed in more detail below and reflect a model of phased induction. Resources are available in the web link provided (www.he academy.ac.uk/3191.htm).

Cultural/administration

A short, structured introduction includes aspects of acclimatisation to HE and advice about the use of the virtual learning environment. The remainder of the session is student-led and involves discussion of the challenges faced in coming to Bournemouth and how these have been resolved. This demonstrates that students are not alone and especially helps if students find the transition to university, or separation from home, particularly difficult.

Personal

This session uses the PDP web site as a framework and helps students gain a better understanding of what and how they are learning. It enables a reflection on their strengths and on areas for personal development. Students are asked to set and discuss goals and action plans which cover:

- personal and social goals
- educational and skills goals
- career and employability goals

The aim of this session is to encourage students to become more effective, independent and confident self-directed learners.

Academic

When assignments are returned some students become anxious about their grades so this is an opportune moment to introduce other aspects of the PDP website, such as reflecting on completed work and goal-setting for future assignments. Other academic issues of concern, such as Harvard referencing can also be discussed and addressed within this forum.

Employment/real working environment

Part of the first year experience within the hospitality programmes centres around the real working environment and therefore aspects such as motivation and team-building are key areas that need to be covered. Employers want well-rounded students and graduates who are motivated, demonstrate a willingness to learn and can adapt to organisational needs. A section on the PDP web site explores effective learning from the work place and this forms the basis for discussion within this session.

Career/placement

As students start to consider progressing to the second year, thoughts will naturally turn to placement. The last strand of personal tutor input therefore focuses on opportunities which are available and encourages students to reflect on the wider agenda of a career within the hospitality industry.

Having this structured delivery by the personal tutor will enable a sense of community within the group, rapport with the tutor and a feeling of identity, as well as building a culture of learning from day one. PDP can be seen to be explicit within this framework. In order to ensure the success of the project, research has shown that personal tutors need support (Wright, 2005). The staff meet on a regular basis and are supported by the programme leader. Resource support is given both through contact time for tutors and some staff development.

In addition, there is still retention of the present culture of open door 'Stop and Knock' tutorial support for issues that are inappropriate for airing in a group situation. Previous research (Hartwell and Farbrother, 2004) showed that students like the opportunity to go to who they wanted to when they wanted to, and whilst this was often the personal tutor, in some instances other staff were involved.

Methodology and analysis

The core of this research is the student experience. Focus groups were conducted with first year students, using a purposive sampling approach that is directed and data collected until saturation point, thereby giving credibility to the study. A research protocol was developed, informed from a review of the relevant literature and previous research conducted at Bournemouth University, with the main issues around tutor support being explored. Spontaneous dialogue was encouraged and covered themes considered important to respondents. At the end of the first term of study focus groups lasting approximately half an hour were held in a seminar room. Students were representative of the first year Hospitality cohort and included men (n=30) and women (n=40). Semi-structured interviews were conducted with the personal tutors (n=5) in their offices to gather relevant information which was pertinent to the study.

Analysis was completed by NUD*IST (Non-numerical Unstructured Data Indexing Searching and Theorising), a computer-assisted, qualitative data analysis software package. Coding was directed by the literature and based on the conceptual framework, allowing for developing themes to be incorporated. Paired sample t-tests were carried out to determine significant differences ($p \leq 0.05$) between wastage figures for academic years 2003/2004 and 2004/2005.

Findings
Stepping Stones

Students reported that they found the site answered many of the questions they had about coming to university and helped them to develop a better understanding of what would be required of them. They felt that it was focused and directed, and a useful information gateway. They also felt more individualised and less like a 'number', many positive comments were made about a 'caring', 'concerned' institution. The task set to be completed for induction week was a useful 'wake up call' and enabled them to prepare for a personal tutor-led session. Some refinements are required, such as making the self profiling questionnaire shorter and more precise but the overall opinion was enthusiastic. It was suggested that the site was as beneficial to parents as to students and acted as a reassurance that the institution was committed to student support. As one student said: '...my mum used it as much as me'.

Evaluation of site-usage demonstrated that there were significantly more hits than students, indicating a revisiting of the information posted. A surge of interest was identified at 'A' level result publication and prior to the deadline of completion of the task.

Personal Tutors

Feedback from staff and students raised a number of justifications for having a formal personal tutoring system in place. These need to be balanced against the cost in resources, both in setting up and in running such an initiative. Key areas for justification are:

■ *Personal contact before a crisis*

Students frequently do not attend tutorials voluntarily until it is too late. A proactive strategy was welcomed by both students and staff, having personal contact and a friendly face can often alleviate a crisis ... 'yes a special relationship has developed and we always say Hi around the campus' (tutor).

■ *Fostering a sense of 'belonging' and establishing a 'friendship group'*

Students leaving home and coming to any new environment can feel isolated, nervous, unsure and that they really want to belong. Having tutor groups gives that identity very early on. Our research found that group identity was formed in induction week. It was also found that each group established a very quick bond with the tutor who had looked after them during that time.

■ *Easing transition HE*

Personal tutors can identify coping strategies for students and help in terms of reassurance, with transition to HE and acclimatisation to HE.

■ *Small-scale discussion forum and an ability to feed back directly to staff*

Having tutorials in groups rather than one-to-one prompted a whole range of discussions. Fringe discussions of this type either did not take place or used up seminar time in timetabled subjects. Although students use Peer Assisted Learning (PAL) as the opportunity for small-scale discussion, staff are absent from these sessions and feedback can be misinterpreted. Students valued the interactive nature of the personal tutor structure.

■ *Head on approach to communicate issues and goal setting*

Having access to small groups of students, or individuals outside of the normal communication forums of notice boards and emails, allows for a more personalised approach to motivating students appropriately.

■ *Support student self-management*

Self-management is a weak area in the first year: this research has found that some students need to be encouraged to self-manage their new-found freedom. Young students miss teacher/parent discipline and attaining self-management is a gradual process that can also be encouraged through attendance-monitoring and following up weaknesses in these areas.

> ... even got admissions of poor time management for their assignments and have worked with them to identify better strategies for next time (tutor)

> ... personal tutors make you feel more focused and motivated (student)

■ *Support for skills gap from formative feedback opportunities*

Giving formative feedback and enabling students to reflect on their learning gives them the opportunity to find gaps in their skills and knowledge. The PDP framework enables students to develop a positive attitude to learning throughout life. With support in reflecting on skills gaps, then helping the students set objectives to fill the gaps, they will be kept on track.

■ *Cheaper to retain than recruit*

This is perhaps the strongest justification of all. Increasing retention of students across the hospitality courses is paramount. The actions carried out in the first year have resulted in the wastage rate on level C hospitality programmes being reduced from over 40 per cent to 12 per cent in one academic year. The latest figure represents a total of only ten students across all the hospitality programmes and is one of the lowest in the school. During the academic year 2004/05, one first year student left before December 1 and five after. This is a significant reduction compared with previous years. The other four leavers were from across years two, three and four and were due to a number of reasons: no particular pattern emerged. Preliminary results from this academic year 2005/2006 look comparable and suggest that personalised tutoring is a successful strategy.

Discussion

Personal tutoring can be an adjunct to academic tutoring and can support students' learning and development over a crucial period in their first year. If a student development process model, as presented at Figure 1, is considered, the role of personal tutor can be seen to be integral to successful development.

Figure 1: Student Development Process Model
(Source: Bournemouth University, personal communication, 2005)

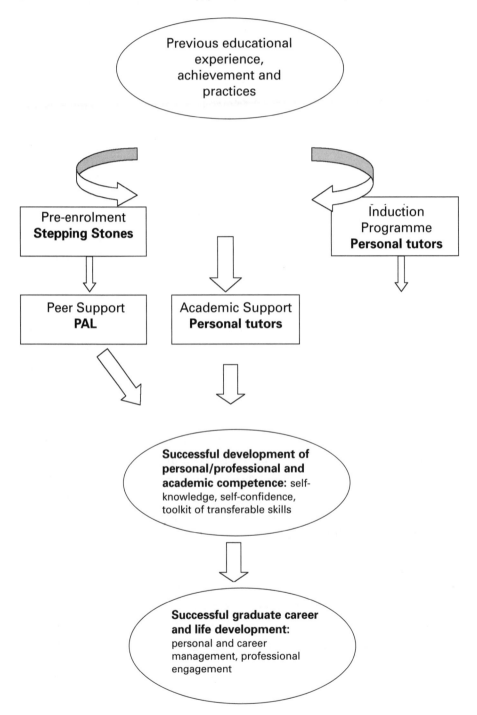

Personal tutoring was traditionally implicit rather than explicit in the School of Services Management, with staff accepting the culture of open door appointments. However, now it is understood that some students need additional assistance and therefore the role of personal tutor has been given a higher profile. The PDP website can be used in this context and is designed to encourage students to reflect on their learning, supported by structured and systematic tutor contact. Broader benefits can be realised by students from more diverse backgrounds, such as the wider community, both nationally and internationally. Focus on enhancing the first year experience is potentially important, in view of the challenges of recruitment and retention. It is intended that the personal tutoring system will not only reduce wastage through withdrawals but will also, due to its coverage, reduce the number of fails across the first year and subsequent years as the cohort moves through the programmes of study. Key elements, as perceived and relating to evidence based practice, have been pre-induction contact via Stepping Stones, continued personal tutor-input through induction, the Peer Assisted Learning scheme and the curriculum model of personalised tutoring using PDP as a framework. From an institutional perspective this strategy meets with targets set for aspects of employability, as identified by the Skills Plus project (Knight and Mantz-Yorke, 2004). A diagrammatic representation of the interface with personal tutors is presented in Figure 2. Enhancing the first year experience is seen as fundamental to the goal of producing a support structure that aids the development of employability beyond a student's academic tutoring. Within student progression towards the successful realisation of personal, professional and academic competence, a support framework, as has been described, is essential.

Conclusion

External and internal stimuli were the drivers for this research. Quality enhancement in HE is a strategic issue for all institutions and there was a high convergence of views from staff that personalised tutoring is an emerging priority, due to agendas of widening participation, student diversity and employability. A framework is required that is sensitive to, and reflective of, student needs, proposing a minimum entitlement of tutor contact. The demand for and real benefits of timely and effective feedback have been highlighted. A cost-effective group-based model, structured into the timetable was considered the best option within the hospitality programmes.

Impending policy and practice will be informed and directed by results from this research. Stepping Stones encourages prospective students to have a

Figure 2: Diagrammatic representation of personal tutor interface

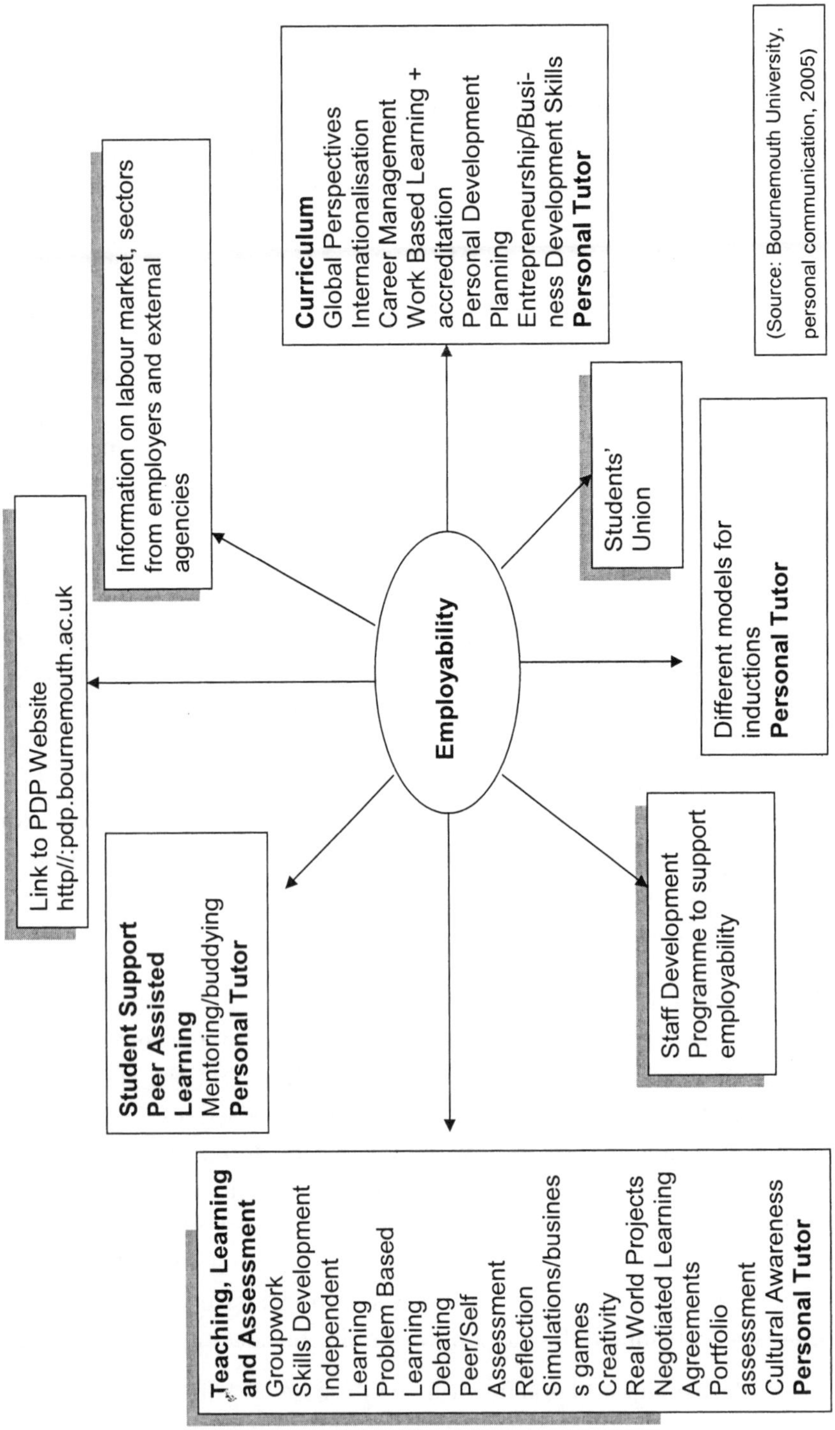

Information on labour market, sectors from employers and external agencies

Link to PDP Website
http//:pdp.bournemouth.ac.uk

Curriculum
Global Perspectives
Internationalisation
Career Management
Work Based Learning + accreditation
Personal Development Planning
Entrepreneurship/Business Development Skills
Personal Tutor

Employability

Students' Union

Different models for inductions
Personal Tutor

Student Support
Peer Assisted Learning
Mentoring/buddying
Personal Tutor

Staff Development Programme to support employability

Teaching, Learning and Assessment
Groupwork
Skills Development
Independent Learning
Problem Based Learning
Debating
Peer/Self Assessment
Reflection
Simulations/business games
Creativity
Real World Projects
Negotiated Learning Agreements
Portfolio assessment
Cultural Awareness
Personal Tutor

(Source: Bournemouth University, personal communication, 2005)

positive relationship with the university and their learning outcomes. Moreover, personal tutors enhance the effectiveness and efficiency of delivering the first year experience. This then allows for the development of employability attributes, skills and qualities. In the future it is recommended that institutional codes of practice and guidelines for personal tutors are produced to provide a comprehensive series of system-wide principles and an authoritative reference point. These documents will also demonstrate a statement of good practice and standards.

Acknowledgements
The authors would like to acknowledge all the first year tutors who participated in this project and enabled the research to progress. Thanks also to Chris Keenan, who introduced the concept of Stepping Stones.

7

Putting students first: Developing accessible and integrated support

Liz Marr and Sheila Aynsley-Smith

Introduction

Within the context of a mass system of higher education, where there is increasing pressure on staff to be all things to all people, personal, face-to-face contact between tutors and students can become a luxury which only the persistent can achieve. Yet we know that personal contact is key in the fight against attrition and in ensuring student success.

At Manchester Metropolitan University, where there has been a tradition of local support via personal tutors and central delivery of student services, we have become increasingly aware of the challenges in managing support and in delivering a quality service to students. As a result of an internally-funded retention and student support project (Marr and Willmott, 2004) in the Faculty of Humanities, Law and Social Science, a system of faculty-based Student Support Officers (SSOs) was piloted and has now been rolled out across the whole University. The SSOs provide generic and proactive support to students within their faculties, bridging the relationship between academic tutors and specialist student services This chapter discusses the context in which the need for change was identified, examines some alternative models of student support and outlines the genesis and purpose of the SSO role. We then describe the pilot project and the rationale for the roll-out, highlighting the advantages of this model over traditional approaches to student support.

Background

Of all the contextual factors impacting on our experiences with students, the policy of widening participation has come under most attack, producing rhetoric around the notion of a new student and contributing to a deficit model of such students. The new student is conceptualised as having one or more identifiable features, such as being non-traditional, mature, first generation, ethnic minority, disabled (for a more comprehensive list see Knutt *et al*, 2005) is argued to have poor qualifications, usually in vocational subjects, and is more likely to fail to progress beyond the first year of their studies than a traditional student. Whatever the reality, we cannot deny that there are some notable features rendering traditional practices in higher education difficult to implement effectively. These include a lack of pre-paredness for study in higher education, (possibly engendered by changes in the school curriculum and the shift away from assessment by examination) (Davies and Elias, 2003) and an increase in what is often seen as instrumenta-lism (Marr and Leach, 2005) but is more likely to be pragmatism, engendered by a reduction in financial support, fee increases and the need to study along-side paid employment (Yorke, 1999). This is not to argue for a deficit model for some students but to suggest that these factors are likely to affect all students, not just those who are first generation entrants.

The problem for academic staff is that we are facing such changes in our co-horts, whilst contending with many other developments in the sector. In-creased managerialism and the development of audit requirements and other mechanisms require us to spend more time monitoring our performance, ensuring that we meet benchmarks and adhere to quality standards (Jary, 2002). At the same time we are facing increasing workloads, as academics must now be professional teachers, competent administrators and publishing researchers, as well as generating income from third stream activities.

The introduction of personal development planning (PDP) has effectively acted as a catalyst, throwing into focus not just the pressures on both staff and students but also the need to bring about change in the student/tutor relationship. The necessity to find time to support students in developing employability skills, to reflect on their teaching and learning and to make links between the two has forced many institutions to consider alternative modes of the delivery of academic and pastoral support, particularly when core skills and competencies are also brought into the frame. Thus, debates abound about whether to integrate or develop stand-alone units in the curri-culum, how additional contact time, which is not assessed and does not therefore carry credits, can be resourced and how staff and student engagement in the process can be encouraged (Ward *et al*, 2005). A common approach appears to have been to locate PDP within the personal tutor function, but the lack of any additional time allowance for this purpose raises further questions about the role of personal tutors.

Alternative models of student support

Until recently the contribution of student support services has tended to be viewed as distinct from the learning and teaching process and the tradition of personal tutoring. In 2002, Universities UK (UUK), in conjunction with SCOP (Standing College of Principals) commissioned a project which initiated an investigation of 'the relationship between student support services and student progress and achievement' (UUK, 2002) and illustrated the pivotal role of student support services in promoting a 'culture of achievement', particularly amongst non-traditional students.

The government's 2003 White Paper (DfES, 2003), published within weeks of the UUK report, lent further weight to the importance of provision which 'meets the developing needs of students for new modes of study and delivery of courses as well as pastoral and learning support' (Para 1 45). This is an argument which we have both promoted in the context of an institution which consistently exceeds its widening participation benchmarks and has a long tradition of recruitment of mature, local students and those from a wide variety of cultural, ethnic and social backgrounds (Aynsley-Smith, 2002).

At Manchester Metropolitan University a range of tutoring models has evolved and co-exists within faculties. There are three recognisable structures, each with advantages and disadvantages: our aim was to harvest the best of each for an enhanced support system.

The use of personal tutors traditionally focuses on pastoral rather than academic support. In the standard approach, every student is allocated a tutor in the first year for the duration of their programme. Meetings can be scheduled periodically through the year or students can approach their tutor as required. Advantages are that the student has a constant experience with someone who gets to know them well, students eventually present less frequently and it is easy to resource fairly across a department. However, there is variability in staff attitudes and therefore performance, which usually results in students ignoring their own personal tutor and going to those who are more approachable. It has also been shown that the relationship does not develop well unless the tutor also teaches the student. Without robust and well-supported information systems, it is difficult to find out about the whole student experience, especially in large departments. Implementing personal development planning schemes around this structure is therefore problematic and eventually we tend only to see those students who have problems and are sufficiently confident to present with them.

As an alternative, some departments have established dedicated skills and pastoral support units as part of the curriculum. The personal tutor teaches the tutee, time allocation is formally recognised and resourced and the unit is an ideal location for the personal development plan. Disadvantages of this model are that it takes time out of the curriculum and thus reduces the discipline specific content. Further, the delivery of core skills and competencies are not seen as effective unless they are integrated. Students do not readily buy into anything perceived as 'not what I am here to do'. Add to this that large departments need large numbers of staff with expertise in teaching skills, the lack of any coherent possible follow through in subsequent years of study and the dedicated support unit loses some of its appeal.

With regard to central provision of student support services, there is no single or consistent model in the UK (Grant, 2005). Although the UUK Report (UUK, 2002) cited many examples of good practice and recognised a diversity of approaches, including the value of one-stop shop arrangements, it did not address the issue of physical location to access of services, which can present major challenges in some institutions, due to historical and geographical factors.

There are many compelling arguments in favour of centrally managed and located support services including:

- specialist teams with a shared ethos and operating under professional codes of practice
- consistent management structure, allowing a higher profile, and access to institutional decision-making structures and strategic arenas
- facilitation of sharing good practice, mutual support and staff development

There are also disadvantages, particularly in a large organisation. Students and staff may be unaware of the availability or remit of such services and students may slip through the net. If services lack visibility or immediacy, students may experience both practical and psychological barriers in accessing them. Staff may not be adequately aware of referral mechanisms and there is minimal scope for discreet intervention from central services in a mass student environment.

Manchester Metropolitan University (MMU) context

The University has a large student population, distributed across seven major campuses within a 40 mile radius. In 2004/5, total student numbers were 32,860 of which 75 per cent were full time and sandwich, 20 per cent postgraduate, half of the students were over 21 and 29 per cent over 24, and a high proportion (59% full time and 80% part time) from the North West of England.

The academic structure of the University is rooted in its seven faculties, the majority of which comprise academic departments. Each faculty has a permanent Dean, supported by a Faculty Registrar, with a strong culture of locally devolved responsibility across a wide range of functions, from site management to student administration and quality assurance. Institutional identity for both staff and students derives locally; central services tend not to be owned, or generally understood, by the majority of staff in regular contact with students.

Student Services at MMU comprise a comprehensive and fairly traditional range of services: Careers, Learning Support (which includes support for disabled students and study skills development), Counselling, Chaplaincy, Student Financial Support, Student Volunteering and Sport. There is close liaison with the Students' Union Advice Centre. Staff are highly professional and committed but the size and structure of the institution militate against their achievement of a significant profile or regular contact with tutors and key influencers.

Within this context the institution has traditionally met benchmarks for retention but it is recognised that, as with other institutions, the situation is worsening and a number of projects have sought to analyse and address the problem. The aforementioned *Attraction, Preparation and Retention Project* (Marr and Willmott, 2004) confirmed, among many findings, the need for coherent personal tutor systems and decentralised, local support for the work.

Student Support Officers (SSO) – a pilot project

In 2003, the Dean of Humanities, Law and Social Science established a working group on retention, with the remit of exploring the lessons learned from the retention project, devising a personal development-planning strategy for the Faculty and considering interventions which might reduce wastage. Its first decision was to introduce some kind of localised support and to construct a link between personal tutors and central services with coherent, transparent and accessible referral systems.

The first SSO was appointed in November 2003 and line-managed within the faculty by the principal lecturer with responsibility for widening participation and retention. Contractual arrangements reflected those operating in Student Services and the post was established on a support staff pay scale with non-academic conditions of service. (Post-92 universities have tended to retain public sector distinctions and do not generally have academic-related contracts). This put the post-holder on a par with the university's learning support advisers and the initial post-holder had experience of guidance work in a nearby careers service. As a fairly recent humanities graduate, she effectively established empathetic rapport with students; she also provided a non-threatening source of information and conduit for Faculty staff.

Following a concentrated publicity campaign, which included emails and letters to students and staff, posters and visits to staff meetings, a statement of service for both staff and students was drawn up. A consultation room was identified and no-appointment drop-in sessions and referral protocols were set up between academic staff and the SSO, and between the SSO and Student Services. Regular generic study skills sessions were delivered and staff were encouraged to request bespoke sessions, such as time management for dissertation students or specialist induction for part time law students. A database for recording enquiries and interventions was designed to aid evaluation and is now being used as part of a major university-wide project to track the reasons students give when they present for support. In addition to input at clearing and induction, the SSO also began to prepare web-based materials to support the PDP process.

Inevitably, the introduction of SSOs generated some tensions, mainly around communications, confusion over the role of the SSO and some preciousness about boundaries. These necessitated some delicate negotiation but are being overcome by awareness and understanding of the role. Nevertheless, the benefits for both staff and students are manifest. Academic staff rapidly identified the SSO as a useful resource and have been keen to take up bespoke skills sessions and to refer students that hitherto they might have had trouble retaining. They have been keen to engage with the SSO in addressing students' problems and issues, including utilising the SSO as a student's 'friend' in disciplinary hearings. Whilst it is not possible to correlate retention to this specific strategy to the exclusion of all other initiatives, it is clear from our records that student and staff take-up of the services on offer has been widespread. A request for assistance with accommodation problems from a student at another university demonstrates just how far the message went out.

Roll-out

In the light of the success of the SSO pilot, the Dean of the Faculty in which the pilot was based, and the Head of Student Services secured agreement in 2004 from the central decision-making forum, Directorate, that Faculty student support officers should be appointed across the University, each to be funded by the relevant faculty. Despite the relatively modest salary offered, the posts attracted a high number of good applicants. Strict adherence to the essential criteria, particularly 'experience of designing and delivering study skills' effectively focused the selection process and narrowed the field. All candidates took up post between June and September 2005. One Faculty, which was undergoing restructuring, deferred the process until early 2006.

The rigour of the selection process, combined with the innovatory nature of the posts, produced six high calibre appointees, who match the character and ethos of the faculty to which they are appointed. Their prior experience varies; with one exception (a Connexions adviser), all had experience of working in higher education, complemented respectively by teaching in HE, FE, secondary education and by undertaking research or project work. They have formed a cohesive and self-supporting team, contributing complementary strengths and prior experience. Building on the foundations of the pilot, they have developed consistent referral systems and databases and are undertaking a guidance qualification. Each has made a significant impact in their faculty, despite differing accounting relationships and expectations. They have become an immediate and identifiable source of referral for tutors, thus minimising lack of awareness of services and redirection to other sites. Inevitably, the SSOs themselves undertake much informal referral but students are less likely to become lost in the process. In collaboration with Student Services, they have developed study skills programmes and have also organised activities to promote support services.

Student Services have identified link representatives and convene termly fora. SSOs are included in Student Services training events and there is mutual participation in team meetings. Some professional anxieties still remain, particularly around boundaries, which are both a challenge and an opportunity; regular communication is crucial.

Justification of changes and comparison with traditional approaches

Although there is a clear expectation in MMU that all students have access to a personal tutor, arrangements vary considerably, reflecting local traditions and policies and the nature, size and level of the programmes so that the concepts of year tutor, personal tutor, and dissertation supervisor, may address the same requirement in different areas. The way in which the role is discharged depends also on local interpretation, personal interest and time availability. Notwithstanding, in the eight years during which Quality Assurance Agency (QAA) subject reviews prevailed, there was consistent awarding of the highest score of 4 for the Student Support and Guidance element.

Many departments have compiled handbooks specifically for personal tutors, with advice, references and referral sources. In reality some tutors keep this resource readily available, are aware of the sources for referral and are proactive in supporting students, whilst others will see the role as an additional and burdensome element of their workload. The variability in approach can be summed up in the following quote from a student who was interviewed about support in the Faculty of Humanities, Law and Social Science, before the introduction of the SSO:

> Tutors, I've had a mixture. I did have one that I found terribly unfriendly and quite disinterested and it made me feel pretty down actually ... but I've had some fantastic tutors as well who have been very encouraging ...

According to Lago and Shipton (1999), 'the underlying intentions of tutoring are geared towards enabling students to achieve, to learn successfully, both academically as well as judgementally'. In a system of mass higher education this responsibility can no longer remain the sole province of the personal tutor; it has to be shared with dedicated service providers and has to be accessible and flexible. The SSOs are not appointed to replace the role of the personal tutor, but to enhance, complement and demystify. They have the scope and the position to become well-known locally, to be owned and to absorb and exemplify the values and ethos of their faculty and to understand the nature of the programmes and academic disciplines.

The value of this provision is perhaps best evidenced through the feedback from staff and students at the end of the first year of the pilot and the SSO's own evaluation of the humanities, law and social science provision. In terms of retention, only one student withdrew from the University, following contact with the SSO since the launch of the project and over 70 per cent of the students who contacted the SSO progressed onto the next stage of their course.

The main queries students presented with were course related – issues such as re-sitting, course changes, study and module options, course applications and non-attendance made up the highest percentage of enquiries. Study skills enquiries followed this closely, with students booking one-to-one sessions to hone their skills in a range of areas, including time management, effective reading and academic writing.

Staff have also responded positively to the initiative, highlighting a number of benefits, summarised by one academic as follows:

> Students have now got someone to go to who understands their particular needs but is still independent of the department. The fact that the service is available says something very reassuring to our students about the commitment to student support in this faculty (even if they don't actually make personal use of the SSO). Staff have someone to liaise with and to advise them on embedding study support, instead of it being just one more thing we would otherwise have to try and do for ourselves.

Although, currently, the SSOs are thinly-spread within their own faculties, there is scope for further extending this arrangement. Advantages over the more *ad hoc* personal tutoring system include:

- separation from teaching responsibilities, allowing dedicated time and availability
- clear line management arrangements, providing formal induction, review and accountability
- ease of access to relevant staff development activities
- informed collaboration and consultation with specialist student services

The establishment of these posts has facilitated targeted, proactive support, which would not previously have been appropriate or deliverable from the more remote central services or over-burdened personal tutors. Examples include: immediate contact with a student who was victim of a crime (i.e. crisis intervention); early identification of support mechanisms for students entering HE from care; local monitoring of the implementation of support arrangements for disabled students' learning – in addition to providing accessible, discipline-related academic guidance.

The formation of a team has engendered a strong sense of professionalism, enabling discussion, reflection (both personal and team) and evaluation of practice, in a way which would not be practicable for the more isolated personal tutor. The requirement to undertake a guidance qualification ensures that SSOs act appropriately and in accordance with relevant codes of practice.

Although the initiative derived from prevailing HE concerns about retention, it reflects current tends in the school sector (DfES, 2005) where teaching staff are being freed up to concentrate on the curriculum, with administrative and pastoral responsibilities being undertaken by staff better placed to do so.

Conclusions

Although at the time of writing we are in the early stages of the full roll-out, the initiative has become embedded so quickly that the role of SSO is now routinely referred to in all strategic decisions relating to such issues as support for students, retention and learning and teaching. Indeed, a recent request for internal funding for a retention project was rejected on the grounds that it made no reference to the SSOs in the project plan. The many benefits of the scheme have already been highlighted but it is worth mentioning one more way in which the SSO will make a difference to the personal tutor role. Personal development planning has many manifestations but the minimum requirements are for a scheme which supports students in developing and reflecting on their learning. Much of this support is ideally given by a personal tutor but the often generic nature of some activities lends itself to central provision. In humanities, law and social science, the SSO is currently working with the developers of the PDP and eportfolio schemes to provide content, tools, materials and resources (physical and electronic) to which personal tutors can direct their students. Although central services have always had the expertise to provide such support, the distributed nature of the organisation has rendered it difficult to access. The role of SSO is bridging the gaps, enabling us to provide a genuinely joined-up support service for students.

8

Creating a network of student support

Barbara Lee and Alan Robinson

Introduction

At the heart of the system of student support is the desire to help students to take advantage of and benefit from their time in higher education. As academics we consider that our core role in student support is to facilitate a student's full engagement in the learning process, whilst recognising that for the student, the academic staff are only one source of support that students have to access to. Our research has shown us that students want to manage their support network, to understand fully how to access services when they need them, and to choose the person they find most appropriate to support them at that time.

This chapter shows how research helped to develop our understanding of the need for an integrated and holistic system of student support and the process of institutional change that was necessary for us to create an approach in which academic and support staff work together under a banner of *Students 1st*, to deliver a timely and effective network of student support.

Reviewing the original system for student support

Southampton Solent University, previously Southampton Institute, has more than 11,000 full time students studying on an extensive portfolio of undergraduate degrees, higher national diplomas and foundation degrees, together with a wide range of taught and research postgraduate degrees, professional education and short courses. Our learning and teaching strategy and academic infrastructure is geared to the needs of an increasingly diverse student intake: as such we are concerned to have effective systems in place to support our students.

In 2000 two student groups, as part of a final year project, were asked to investigate perceptions amongst fellow students of the personal tutoring system then in operation. This was a standard system of personal tutoring in which a group of students was allocated to an individual academic who acted as their personal tutor. The student researchers reported that students had a variable experience of tutoring and that where a tutor was not helpful students experienced difficulties in identifying and approaching the appropriate person for support. However, it was also clear that students actively rejected a proactive model of tutoring, in which the tutor scheduled and set an agenda for meetings at regular intervals, stating a clear preference to establish and manage their own support network. What they sought from tutors was a more consistent and clearly signposted system of support.

Looking at the situation from the perspective of the students, it is apparent that the tutor is only one part of their network of support. The University's *Learner Experience and Achievement Project* (Lim, 2002) survey for 2001/2 illustrates how much students advise and help each other and how important this is to them. When seeking academic advice, 65 per cent of students first approached other students on the course, with only 46 per cent of Level 1 students going to their personal tutor. When looking for non-academic advice, 54 per cent turned to other students on the course and only 8 per cent reported approaching their personal tutor.

Although students want to manage their network of support, it is traditionally part of a personal tutor's role to understand institutional systems and to facilitate student access to specialist help (Owen, 2002). This potentially leaves students who have not formed a working relationship with a tutor adrift in a system they do not understand at a time when they need help. If this student has also not managed to form the beginnings of a network of friends, they will be particularly at risk. Barker (2000) reports that 'a significant minority of students are clinically lonely' and gives loneliness as the third highest reason given by students for dropping out. Our own research also shows that students have a significant role to play in each other's networks of support. So the tutor not only needs to introduce the student to the University and its systems but also to help students to get to know each other. At the simplest level, knowing another student to sit with in a lecture helped students to manage the first few weeks in their new learning environment better.

The learning process may begin to break down for a number of academic and/or non-academic reasons and as the difficulty impacts further on their studies the students' understanding of how the system of support may be accessed is crucial. Our research has shown us that students did not understand the full extent of the network of support available (tutors, central services, faculty support staff, Students' Union etc.), or were often simply unable to find their personal tutor at the time of need. This led to students turning away disheartened, believing that the system did not have a place for them. Eaton and Bean (1995) point out that those students who are at risk may be the very same students who are the least visible. Indeed the question arises: do students leave quietly, testing the institution through non-attendance to find out whether or not the institution notices or cares?

It became clear from our internal research that we needed to pay attention to helping students find their way through the system better and to assist them in forming effective systems of support for themselves. Students need help to 'manage the transition into higher education better' and to 'induct them properly into what HE is about' (House of Commons Education and Employment Select Committee, 2001). This induction is a continuing process, as students' needs and demands on institutional resources will inevitably change as they progress through their course of study. In-house research, underpinned and supported by published research, influenced a move towards a holistic view of student support (Robinson, 2002). The system was devised to fit alongside the learning process, as opposed to being just an add-on: frequently it is only when something goes wrong that the learning process breaks down. These considerations led to the development of the Student Support Network, which was designed to be an integral part of the learning process, and to offer a range of timely interventions according to the needs of the students.

A proactive/reactive approach

The principles of the Student Support Network were that it should be seen as:

- providing a clear point of reference for students who are trying to find advice and help on an issue
- seeking to encourage the formation of student work/support groups
- providing appropriate learning support when students face academic difficulties
- giving first stop support to students who wish to discuss personal difficulties
- helping students to make informed choices

- maintaining a clear record of student progress and issues affecting this (eg monitoring and reporting non or poor attendance and levels of engagement)
- giving a structure in which students are supported in their progress as reflective adult learners.

Two key elements are central to the delivery of this set of principles. One is to have an effective and ongoing induction for all students, which both introduces them to the institution and encourages the building of the friendships and working relationships that fill out their personal support networks. The second is to provide a visible access point for all support services, underpinned by a joint training programme for academic and support staff so that all members of the institutional support network understand each other's roles.

Induction should be seen not as a one-week event but as an ongoing process involving students working together to make sense of their new academic environment (Lowe and Cook, 2003) and to encourage social and academic integration (Tinto, 1993). Induction activities are a key point for an institution to be proactive, as support at the beginning of a student's experience of higher education is critical (Yorke and Thomas, 2003; Thomas, 2002). As the needs and expectations of each student will vary it is essential to ascertain these on entry and to monitor them throughout the course. More importantly, once needs are identified there must be an attempt to meet them, whilst also aligning the expectations of students with those of the university.

Through Spiral Induction programmes, via student-centred, individual and group learning activities, staff can monitor the level of engagement of students and be proactive in targeting support. In this way students are encouraged to take responsibility for their own learning within a network of structured support. The team of support tutors fulfils all the standard functions of a personal tutor. These tutors are members of the academic staff with an interest in student welfare; they work together with administrative staff and university student services to provide a coherent and open support system which aims to be accessible at the point of need.

To enable students to access the support system independently, visible access points were created under the banner of *Students 1st*. Staff at these access points have been trained to facilitate the student in finding the appropriate person to help them. All staff, whether academic, administrative or within student support services, who were involved in the new system, underwent joint training. If academic and administrative staff do not know that certain services exist, it will not occur to them to refer a student onwards. Similarly by listening to the issues concerning administrative and academic staff, student services were able to understand both staff concerns and training needs better.

Students 1st: Creating a visible and timely system of student support

Setting these new systems in place required change within the University and occurred as part of major development in creating an academic framework for the University. The process of creating the academic framework represented a participatory, mature and dynamic approach to educational change management within the University, involving input from a wide range of staff. Its introduction followed consultation within faculties, prior to detailed consideration and approval by the Academic Board. The Academic Framework now represents a co-ordinated set of policies aimed at enabling Southampton Solent University to develop, in a principled and consistent way, the educational provision and learning experience it offers to students.

The process of change is carefully monitored and its impact and effectiveness continues to be evaluated. This helps to ensure that the essential elements for student success are consistent and accessible for all students, at all levels. The Framework has been developed and implemented in a considered and phased manner. Phase One was launched in 2001-02 and resulted in approval by Academic Board of the Student Support Network (SSN), and Spiral Induction, in May 2002 for implementation in September 2002 with the Students 1st branding being introduced in 2003.

Students 1st is distinctive in that it coordinates all parts of the network of student support, including the Students' Union, and provides an integrated approach to learning which aligns the institutional culture and environment with the learning activities undertaken. The linked component parts of Students 1st comprise: Student Support Network (SSN), Spiral Induction Programme (SIP), Students 1st, providing information, advice and guidance points which are explained below.

By developing and investing in new kinds of support that are explicitly linked to learning and that enable targeting of resources more efficiently and effectively, we have already significantly improved retention rates without increasing the operational costs of this support.

Student Support Network (SSN)

The SSN has an innovative team-based approach which is designed to integrate student support across the university and to be pro-active in identifying and responding to student needs. It integrates support into the curriculum. Academics who are interested in this area work within the course team as Support Tutors, they engage in spiral induction activities and identify themselves as a point of contact within the system. Students can access Support Tutors, who either resolve the issue or identify a need for referral, all with the central aim of helping the student to engage with – or return to – the learning process. Once needs are identified, the expertise of a range of staff across the institution can be harnessed to channel support to the student.

Spiral Induction Programme (SIP)

Our initial emphasis in developing the spiral induction programme was to work with the first year students who are in transition into higher education (Collins and Lim, 2003a) and therefore in the greatest need of induction work. SIP provides structured learning opportunities delivered by academics who have been trained in the role of Support Tutors. SIP actively involves students in helping and supporting each other. It provides the stimulus and safety net for students to make the transition from passive into active learners.

An essential element of the initial spiral induction programme (SIP) with first year students is to provide an opportunity for students to work on collaborative activities in an informal manner with as many of their fellow students as possible. As Robson (1998) suggests, collaborative activities facilitate levels of peer support and peer learning which are not offered by teacher-centred approaches. These groups are inducted into how to help each other to access the university's safety net of support. The informal nature of these sessions helps students to adjust to the requirements of the university's teaching and learning environment, to deal with change, and to develop generic communicative and interpersonal skills.

The SIP programme is now being developed further. It acts as the launch pad for Reflections, a core element in the personal development planning (PDP) programme, and is moving on to create programmes to help students with issues such as career planning, which concern them as they progress through their undergraduate studies.

Students 1st – Information, advice and guidance points

In September 2003 the Students 1st and the Information Centre and Assistive Technology Centre, after a major refurbishment and relocation of central student support services, were placed in a clearly visible and central location. In addition University wide Students 1st branding and associated signage was introduced. The Students 1st logo creates a simple coherent image based on the customer, rather than organisational needs, and makes it clear to students, staff and the outside community that we intend to deliver a high level of service and that we put students first. All points throughout the University where a student can drop in with a support query carry the Students 1st sign. This includes not only the Central Information Centre but also the Students' Union Advice Centre, faculty help desks, finance service, study assistance, Accommodation Centre, Library and learning and study support teachers. Any person who is on duty at one of these points has been trained and fully understands the support network so that they know where to refer students if they cannot answer their query themselves. The objective is to be able to pass students on directly from that one query to the person who can best help them. In this way the network aims to put individual learners in touch with those who are best able to provide the help that they need, when they need it.

Conclusions – confidence in the approach

The process of change is not yet complete. The need to develop further PDP and Careers Education within the curriculum has meant that spiral induction needs to progressively move with the student throughout their specific programme of study. Engagement monitoring, which incorporates attendance monitoring, is being developed as a better method of identifying students who may be at risk. The timely data on student engagement in the SIP activities is used diagnostically to fine-tune the management of student learning.

As part of the university's learning, teaching and curriculum development strategy, our Research Unit have evaluated the implementation and impact of both the SSN and the SIP with students and staff, using a mixed methodology of surveys and interviews (Collins and Lim, 2003b). The Learner Experience and Achievement Project (LEAP) has recorded data on an annual basis and between 2001 and 2003 has shown a steady improvement in students' management of the process of transition into higher education. Fewer students now report academic problems in transition (31.2% in 2001, 30.0% in 2002 declining to 20.9% in 2003). The social difficulties associated with the move to higher education appear to have also diminished (14.2% in 2001, 15.1% in 2002 declining to 7.2% in 2003). In addition, fewer students have problems with the transition between levels (23.4% in 2001, 19.6% in 2002 declining to 10.1% in 2003)

In each of these categories there is a sharp fall in the number of students experiencing problems with making transitions between 2002 and 2003, which coincided with the introduction of the SSN and SIP, two of the component parts of Students 1st.

The surveys also show that there is a significant increase in students commending the induction process, commenting that is helps them to get to know other students and meet staff on a less formal basis, as well as creating opportunities to learn about systems and resources, and to reflect on and improve their study skills. Comments from staff in the study illustrate that Students 1st enables all parts of the network to communicate and share issues. This means that most problems are dealt with at the point of contact when students make their initial approach for support, so that they don't have to explain their problem again. Compared with previous years there is a significant increase in the number of students who know where to go for support and information.

Other groups also evidence the effectiveness of the new SSN. Course teams through the annual course monitoring process have highlighted the significant contribution to enhancing the student experience and aiding retention made by the Student Support Network and Spiral Induction Programme. The university's Retention Working Group have also reported that the initiatives to improve in-level retention (a measure of non-completion during the year) have been increasingly successful, rising from a baseline figure of 92.3 per cent in 2000/1 to 94.9 per cent. Close monitoring and support of students at risk through the various component parts of Students 1st has played a significant part in achieving this success.

So although the process of monitoring and improving the network of student support continues, the evidence assures us that the process of change has been worthwhile. We have moved from a system that was variable in delivery and reactive in approach, to one that supports all students in their move into confident independent learning in higher education.

9

Platoons to encourage social cohesion amongst a large and diverse undergraduate population

Peter Hill

The Background

When I first became an undergraduate, there were thirty students in my course's first year. When I did a masters degree there were almost eighty. For both, we had a common room dedicated to our course. I knew everybody in my year and they knew me. We supported each other, with only the occasional quarrel.

At the Business School of the university where I work now, there are over 700 undergraduates in the first year. Although they are attached to eight different courses, the first year modules are roughly the same for them all; for the first year they're effectively on one big course.

They can't possibly know all of their peers. But has the sheer size of the programme deprived them of the sort of peer group support I had?

As well as the size of the operation, there are other factors. Students are now more dependent on part time work to support their studies. They are also more diverse in culture, ethnicity and home country than they were a generation ago. With the widening HE participation rate, there are more who represent the first generation of their family to attend university. So there is less communality of background among the students than there once was, making it less likely that a student in difficulty will receive peer group support.

There is no common room for undergraduates on our campus, although one is promised.

Is isolation and lack of peer support a contributory cause of drop out or failure?

This was the question we sought to address in 2004/5. It does not allow direct research; we can never show full causation and drop outs are notoriously in-accessible to follow-up questioning. Instead, we decided to change the deployment of the first year to enhance peer group interaction.

First, we needed to know how isolated students might be. Modules are taught by lecture and seminar; the lectures are large, containing up to 330 students but the seminars are in groups with a maximum of 24. Each student undertakes four modules per semester, with a weekly lecture and seminar in each.

In the worst case, a student would see 92 different faces every week; (4 x 23) in her/his seminars. If Alice sees Beth in two different seminars, we call this a common fellow (CF). Alice would have two common fellows if she saw Beth in three seminars, or Beth in two seminars and Charlotte in two seminars.

A score of 69 (3 x 23) common fellows would indicate that Alice saw the same people in all of her four seminars: one CF point for each student she sees in a second seminar. So since Alice sees Beth in four seminars this makes three CF points. Three points also for Charlotte, Diana and so on through to Xenia, the twenty fourth member of the group.

The actual results for the last year before the experiment were:

Number of common fellows	Percentage
0	22.3%
1	19.9%
2	17.9%
3	13.2%
4	11.5%
5	7.0%
6	4.3%
7	1.2%
8	2.1%
9	0.5%

It's easy to see that there is a high degree of fragmentation; over a fifth of students met no other fellow student in class more than once a week. A socially well-adjusted and motivated student can overcome this but are all students socially well-adjusted and motivated? We don't know them; we don't select by interview. HE expansion has brought in students from a wider variety of backgrounds. Some are less habituated to HE norms than their predecessors a generation ago. We, the faculty, do not necessarily know the assumptions they may bring to HE.

Yorke (2002) lists certain student circumstances as particularly vulnerable to drop out. These are when:

- students have chosen the wrong programme
- students' lack commitment and/or interest
- students' expectations are not met
- students come from a working class background
- students are mature entrants
- students enter with low academic qualifications
- the quality of teaching is poor
- the academic culture is unsupportive (even hostile) to learning
- students experience financial difficulty
- demands of other commitments supervene (Yorke, 2002:35)

If Yorke is right, even in part, then the intakes of universities lower down the league tables, often post-1992 institutions, probably contain more of the vulnerable type of student he describes. We certainly could critique this list: for example we do not know how many students have chosen the wrong programme or whether anybody knows whether they chose the right programme. Would I be happier or richer if I had read Anthropology instead of English? But if there is such a thing as the right programme, it would follow that students from better schools would get better advice on their choice of course and that students from families with a history of HE would get more family help with their choice than students who are the first generation of their families to go to university.

Most London universities and colleges have another problem: they suffer from being what Joad (1945) called 'a commuter University'. Students have to travel relatively long distances to attend; because of this they are not immersed in an educational or intellectual culture.

Discontent about one particular aspect of the study situation can spread into a more general dissatisfaction that leads to drop out or failure; the lack of academic or social integration in Tinto's (1975) model or the gaps between service providers' perceptions and those of customers in the work of Zeithaml, Parasuraman and Berry (1990).

I have shown elsewhere (Hill, 2004) that students increasingly regard themselves as customers but that teaching staff do not recognise this. Some of the problems experienced within undergraduate programmes may be explained by perceptual mismatch; we can partially cure them by addressing these differential perceptions. Perceptual mismatch is likely to be greatest where students have poor habituation to the norms of HE, ie where students know neither what to expect nor what is expected of them. Where expectations are uninformed, false assumptions may take their place, and since many assumptions on either side are not articulated – as is the nature of assumptions – there is little awareness of the mismatch until it becomes a perceptual gulf.

The worst-case student:

- has just scraped the entry requirements for the course and is unsure about whether they have the intellectual capabilities to succeed
- has not attended a college or school where university-level study skills are supported
- is relatively poor and has to undertake paid work to support studying
- comes from a family with no experience of university, hence no or misleading information/support;
- lives a long way away, not near other students and has to commute expensively and uncomfortably in rush hour
- has a timetable which is widely spaced
- does not have an intuitive grasp of the learning material
- is uncomfortable reading textbooks written in academic language
- lacks assertiveness or the ability to ask for help.

How the problem affected individuals

Let's follow the path of the worst-case student, described above. I'll call him Peter, after myself. He will enrol on one of the courses in my school at my university, in 2003. Things may be different in other schools or universities but he won't know that.

Peter arrives for registration and induction. He queues. He attends the induction events. He registers for a timetable by copying down his core modules from a handbook to a form and chooses an option module in the same way. In the first week of teaching Peter attends four lectures in large cavernous lecture halls. If he's lucky, he might recognise somebody he saw at induction; if not, then not. He's quite shy; he won't initiate contact. He's told that seminars start in the second week: he's not quite sure what a seminar is because he hasn't been to university before and nor has anybody in his family but he won't ask for fear of sounding stupid.

When seminars start in the second week, Peter finds himself in four seminar groups. In each of these groups there are different people, from different courses, some within the school, some from other schools and faculties. Their motivations are different; their levels of commitment are variable. Peter doesn't see the same faces across his different modules. Although there's discussion in the seminars, it doesn't spill over outside the seminar; people dash off to other classes or to their jobs. Peter has a long distance to commute; he has made no friends and even if he had, there is no common room to meet them in. He goes home each day as soon as he conveniently can.

Peter perceives dimly that something is wrong here; he should be making friends but he isn't. He decides to initiate some social contact. Fearing rejection, he goes where rejection is least likely – to people of a similar ethnic and cultural background. Perhaps these friends sustain him in his study; perhaps they don't; he doesn't see them more than once a week in seminars, so there's a good chance that they won't. Because of the basis on which he's chosen them, they won't broaden his horizons much.

Broadening horizons – the transformation of the individual – have been lost from the national agenda for higher education. The Robbins Report spoke of 'the transmission of a common culture and common standards of citizenship' (1963:7). The Dearing Report (1997) redefined this as how 'to shape a democratic civilised and inclusive society'. Between the times of these two reports the student has moved from someone to be formed to someone who brings a pre-existing formation with them, which is then to be included in society. This development has paralleled the introduction of modular systems and the consequent focus on delivery of learning rather than the shaping of the mind; the commodification of education (Lyotard, 1984; Harvey, 1990). And yet, dare we consider that the transformational role of higher education is dead?

Greater socialisation can promote transformationalism but universities have a much more instrumental reason for promoting it. If Peter makes friends with his peers, two things may follow. First, because he has more motivation for attending, he will attend more, feel more closely associated with the university and thus be less likely to drop out. Secondly, because he has peer group contact he has additional sources of information and support, which means that the university itself needs to provide less support.

Peter is not habituated to HE norms; he does not know what level of work and reading input is required of him; he does not know what he is expected to do, other than pass assignments. He may equate passing assignments with learning and feel supported in that belief by the importance the institution attaches to marks. He may have been briefed at induction but the effect is fleeting. A strong peer group can help in the habituation process at the cost of developing a canteen culture which may be at odds with the objectives of the university itself.

What we did

My university was suffering from drop out and failure; we were shocked by the high degree of fragmentation within the student body. This had evolved over the years of expansion: until we did the calculations we were not aware how potentially isolated students could be.

The logical step was to increase the level of social contact among the students by increasing the number of common fellows from its mean of 2.3 to something approaching the theoretical maximum of 69.

We introduced platoons as an experiment with the 2004 intake of over 550 full time undergraduates to the Business School. The Business School has eight different courses, but the first year for these courses is nearly identical. This consists of six core modules, the same for each course, with two further variable modules which can be remedial (Maths, English), or optional, or course-specific for the smaller, more specialised courses. Each module is taught by large lecture (usually repeated twice in a week) plus many seminar groups limited to 24 students.

Modules are delivered in two semesters, four modules each. Because of the massive size of the mega-modules, they are delivered in both semesters. Many students from outside the Business School take the modules, leading to annual enrolments of sometimes 800.

Until the platooning experiment, the allocation of students to seminar groups was either random or modified self-choice, leading to the high degree of fragmentation described earlier.

We couldn't reserve seminars for one course; that would have given too many part full seminars and with courses of 150 and more, this would still have resulted in a high level of fragmentation. Instead, we programmed students into units of 24, called platoons. Students in the platoons would not necessarily be on the same course but on one of two or three related courses.

Most students had a variable module in the first semester and these modules were not subject to platooning. Thus, every student would have three seminars per week usually with the same 23 students, some of whom they would also meet in their option module. This would give a CF score for each student of 46, plus any CF in the same seminar for the variable module. We put students from outside the school into dedicated seminar groups outside the core teams, with the seminar groups immediately adjacent to the lecture, so they could easily attend events in their home schools.

The logistics of achieving this simple end were horrendously complex. Eventually, we devised a scheme which put students into platoons and also allowed seminars to start in the first week of teaching. In previous years, the first week had contained only lectures until the seminars were sorted out and we suspected that this arrangement had failed to harness the enthusiasm of new starters.

About 95 per cent of incoming full time undergraduates in the school were successfully placed in platoons. There were difficulties when students had compassionate circumstances or had enrolled late, or had somehow missed the correct desk on enrolment, and others caused by the inability of the old student record system to exclude non-platooned students from the groups designated for platoons. It was also difficult to dovetail one of our courses with modules hosted by another school – but we did not expect 100 per cent success on the first implementation.

The first allocation to platoons was intended to last for the first semester and a second allocation was intended for the second semester. The platoons were renamed Core Teams for public consumption; the term 'platoon' was thought to be unnecessarily militaristic.

How results were affected

Academic results from the platooned intake showed an improvement on the previous year. Many improvements in syllabus and teaching were introduced in the year in question. The causes of non-drop out are impossible to measure, as is why some students pass and others don't. Drop out has decreased between the 2003 and 2004 intakes. On one of the two largest courses (BA Business Studies) the percentage withdrawing has dropped from 8 per cent to 4 per cent, and on the other (BA Business Management) from 10 per cent to 2 per cent. With lower numbers, the Economics/Business degrees have reduced drop out from 9 per cent to 3 per cent; the course title has been changed, as has the syllabus in this and other courses. The module pass rate for the platooned year was 81.0 per cent; that for the previous year 76.8 per cent.

So many complexities underlie these figures, such as the effect of modules repeated after failure and the change in syllabi and in teaching methods, including the introduction of problem-based learning.

The scheme continued into academic year 2005/6, with an increased student intake (710) and other changes, some of which were forced by the adoption of a new academic calendar, others as a result of learning from the first implementation.

Monitoring the effectiveness of the changes was an important factor in understanding things about our students that we did not know. Just as we had not noticed the fragmentation of the seminar groups, so there were other things about the students which were at odds with our assumptions about them. This is the sort of perceptual mismatch that underlies the gap analysis model of service delivery of Zeithaml, Parasuraman and Berry (1990).

What we learned from monitoring the scheme

Monitoring the scheme gave us evidence to support the idea that there was a perceptual mismatch between staff and students. One striking example was that when asked to choose their first priority in their study, 56 per cent declared that their first priority was to get a first class degree. Another 11 per cent identified upper second or better as their first priority, making two thirds whose motivation can be defined primarily in terms of mark achievement. This does not only show perceptual mismatch but also the seeds of disappointment and dissent; if the past is a guide, less than 5 per cent will be awarded first class honours.

Very few showed intrinsic motivation (Butler, 1988): only 6 per cent wanted to learn more about their subject as their first priority and only 22 per cent mentioned this anywhere in the top three. A well-paid job outranked an interesting job in the list.

But are these responses as positive as they first seem? If a first-class degree were a means to an end, such as a postgraduate degree, a professional qualification or a well-paid job, the end would show in the responses rather than the means. As it was 69 per cent gave the first class degree as one of their three priorities, 59 per cent the well-paid job, 13 per cent the postgraduate degree and 23 per cent the professional qualification. This means that students want a first class degree for its own sake rather than for the doors it opens. This must stem from the need for high self-esteem, for validation of the self through external recognition of achievement (high grade; high pay). It accords with Covington's (1992) suggestion that there was a mismatch of perceptions between students and academic staff, the former assuming that students' motivations lay in learning, the latter preferring to maintain self-worth. In terms of Maslow's (1954) hierarchy, they are further from the self-actualisation level than we assume.

Two figures show the difference between these students and the traditional image of the student: 60 per cent lived with parents or relatives and 55 per cent had previously attended a college rather than a school. Only 35 per cent had quite a good idea of what to expect at university; the rest had some, little or no idea. There is no association between having little idea of what to expect and having attended a college rather than a school. This again hints at the unhabituated student, less likely to be exposed to peer formation than those living among their fellow students, and less likely to be of the university-going class.

Do they support each other in the way the experiment assumed?

(Referring to the platoon):	Agree or Strongly Agree	Disagree or Strongly Disagree
We study together outside the classroom	53%	24%
We socialise together outside the classroom	60%	20%
We help each other with our assignments	70%	6%
We are friends	68%	6%
I knew some of the members before teaching started	18%	68%

This table suggests that students do support each other. There are the usual definitional difficulties: how can they help each other with assignments without studying together?

What are their sources of peer help?

	I give help to	I receive help from
People in the same group	56%	55%
Both equally	34%	29%
People in other groups	8%	9%
Never happened	3%	8%

	I have been stuck and my fellow students have helped me	A fellow student has been stuck and I have helped him/her
Very often	9.4%	22.2%
Often	33.3%	44.4%
Sometimes	40.9%	30.4%
Rarely	15.2%	1.8%
Never	1.2%	0.0%

	I am most likely to find friends
Within my course	83%
Within my seminar group	82%
With those with whom I share a leisure interest	42%
Within the same ethno-cultural group	35%
Within the same age group	25%
Within the same social class	16%

These figures indicate a dependence on the peer group for both learning and social purposes. Peers therefore have a role in Tinto's (1975) model in both academic and social integration; we might otherwise assume that the peer group plays a role in social integration only. If they help each other as frequently as these figures suggest, then it is the peer group that sets the academic standard, or at least is responsible for the strategic approach to assessment (Entwistle and Ramsden, 1983).

The picture emerging from the survey is of a normative undergraduate arriving from a college which was maybe more impersonal and less of a community than a school, knowing nobody. They socialise, but not much, having an average of seven friends at the end of the first semester and knowing the names of fourteen more – not even all the members of their seminar group. These friends are most likely to be those with whom they share a seminar group, rather than a leisure interest or a demographic similarity.

The students surveyed spend on average 9.8 hours per week on paid work, 11.5 hours on study outside taught classes and 11 hours on social activities. 32 per cent do no paid work; of those who do, the spread is wide with peaks around 15 and 20 hours and a maximum of 40. All these students are officially on full time programmes.

Respondents are more likely to miss lectures than seminars: of the platooned students, the mean number of lectures missed (out of a possible maximum of 48) was 3.9 and the mean number of seminars missed out of 48 was 3.0. Fifteen per cent claimed to have missed no lectures and 23 per cent no seminars.

Do the students see the peer group as a major learning method? The above questions tested socialisation and stuckness reaction (Claxton, 1999); does the peer group also feature proactively? Respondents were asked to rank various learning methods in order of their effectiveness. They were:

lectures
seminars
assigned readings
non-assigned readings
help from my fellow students
doing the assignments
the internet

Six per cent ranked help from their fellow students first, 6 per cent second, 11 per cent third, 11 per cent fourth, 15 per cent fifth and 19 per cent sixth. So 33 per cent gave no ranking at all to the peer group as a learning method. 60 per cent gave no ranking to non-assigned readings; 24 per cent to the internet; 18 per cent to assigned readings; 12 per cent to doing assignments; 8 per cent to lectures. Every respondent rated seminars somewhere in their rankings.

This showed that the peer group isn't seen as a primary learning method like seminars or lectures. It ranks as a support learning method: some students may resort to friends rather than to non-assigned readings. Their in-experience means that they regard the world wide web in a similar way.

Fellow students are not a proactive learning resource; on the basis of the contrast between these two groups of questions they are reactive. Even so, about

23 per cent of the students rated their fellow students amongst the top three learning resources.

What can we conclude?

Before this experiment we had allowed systems to develop which inhibited students' learning by leaving them isolated. The students didn't complain – how could they? They had no comparison point. But the systems had evolved to suit convenient delivery of a complex programme and, like them, we had lost sight of the human factor.

Not all universities or disciplines are similar. In some, this problem won't arise. Seminar fragmentation won't apply in departments and subjects where teaching is, say, in three-hour blocks with no smaller groups.

Our students have changed and we haven't noticed. Tutorials have helped individuals, but tutors' hands are tied unless they notice all the changes, and unless they keep their assumptions about students up to date.

We need to keep monitoring who our students are and we're turning this into a longitudinal study. In the meantime, we're reasonably satisfied that we have to continue to ensure that our students have a sufficiently strong peer group to give and receive support, and are not isolated. The interaction we don't see is more important than the more formal interaction we do see.

10

Strategic approaches to the development and management of personal tutorial systems in UK higher education

Margo Blythman, Susan Orr, Daphne Hampton, Martina McLaughlin and Harry Waterworth

Introduction

This chapter explores our experience, over nine years, of taking a strategic approach to personal tutoring within University of the Arts London. University of the Arts London comprises five colleges and specialises in art, design and communication. It is the biggest art and design education institution in Europe and possibly the world. The chapter outlines the positive development we have been able to achieve in some of the colleges of the university and the tensions and difficulties we encountered. In particular we examine:

- developing appropriate structures and cultures with a particular focus on the role of the tutorial co-ordinator
- relating this work to the wider structures and aims of the university/ college
- harnessing resources
- strategic problems and ways forward

These are set within current policy contexts of widening participation, internal and external quality reviews and increasing focus on the student experience. Additionally, we draw on our experience of how such strategies were developed in further education and the lessons in this for higher education. Our view is that many current strategies around diversity and the student experience have come from FE (Blythman and Orr, 2002) and that the HE sector has a lot to learn from developments in this sector (Green, 2001).

In the second part of the chapter the personal tutorial strategy is explored through a series of related theoretical concepts of cultural capital (Bourdieu, 1997), the space between (Ellsworth, 1997), access and participation (Archer *et al*, 2003; Riddell *et al*, 2005) academic literacies (Grimm, 1999; Lea and Street, 1998; Lillis, 2001;) and micropolitics (Hoyle, 1982; Ball and Rowe, 1991). In conclusion we pull together our practical experience with the underpinning theoretical constructs. We aim to encourage practitioners to appreciate that personal tutorial systems can benefit from personal tutors and managers having a deeper theoretical understanding of educational issues that impinge on the success of personal tutorial systems.

Rationale for our approach

We come from a value position of supporting widening participation, equity and social justice in higher education and see personal tutorial support as a key strategy. We also come from a perspective of micropolitics (Hoyle, 1982) which has led us to explore how things get done around here. This involves considering the position of personal tutoring in relation to access to resources, the institutional agenda, both public and private, and the current focus of institutional energy and related discourse. How does this translate into, or clash with the working practices and values of individual and groups of academic staff.

Developing appropriate structures and cultures

Our starting point was the need to operate across a number of levels. It is useful to think of institutions on three levels: the macro level of the whole institution, the micro level of the individual academic and the less-often discussed meso level (Trowler *et al*, 2005) of the department or course/subject team. At London College of Fashion (LCF) and London College of Communication (LCC) (both colleges of University of the Arts, London) we started to give a focus by setting up a group to produce a tutor handbook. This was an open group that anyone could join but it had senior management support. We quickly realised the importance of the meso level and the need for a middle management structure for tutoring. From FE we brought our experience of developing management structures for personal tutorial systems and had realised that we needed some formal management structure in order to have access to resources and symbolic power. This required a definition of personal tutoring, which became the systematic monitoring and support of individual academic progress across the whole programme. This ensures that, on a continuum of academic to pastoral, tutoring is located much closer to academic. It also meant that we needed a job description for tutors and this new middle management role, and adequate resourcing not only of tutoring itself but the management of tutoring. We were on our way to developing an institutional policy which raised the profile of the project at all levels and in a variety of arenas.

The development of the role of school tutorial co-ordinator was crucial to our strategy. Their main responsibilities are around supporting and monitoring personal tutoring provision within their school. Their remit is as follows:

- ensuring that provision is in place and is properly resourced and roomed
- introducing students at induction to the idea of personal tutorials
- being part of the induction process for new staff
- cascading information both formally and informally through a termly tutor newsletter
- having a presence at school boards of study
- linking with student representatives and university central services for students
- raising awareness of the importance of personal tutoring at every opportunity.

Some key factors for the success of this role include having a culture of student support within the school and university, good relationships with deans of schools, strong links with and support from deans and quality/ learning and teaching managers, good knowledge of the school and how it operates as a community of practice (Wenger, 1998), being able to work with colleagues in a context of using both pressure and support and proper re-sourcing of the role.

Tutorial co-ordinators are able to influence approaches to personal tutoring by working alongside personal tutors over concerns expressed by students about matters such as access to staff. Tutorial co-ordinators can also ensure that the personal tutorial system starts well by making sure that they are in-volved in student induction, helping to bring some consistency to the per-sonal tutoring message, and by developing contacts with student course representatives across the school. They can support individual personal tutors when dealing with difficult student personal tutoring issues. They can help jump-start projects such as student-to-student mentoring. They can also support staff with documenting the personal tutoring process, by working to achieve records that gather the necessary facts in the least laborious way. This experience can then be used to produce case studies for staff development purposes around this role. Another way for the tutorial co-ordinator to support personal tutors is by taking responsibility for the documentation of the whole personal tutorial system for quality review purposes and by helping individual tutors with their own contribution to this written account. This was regarded as invaluable by personal tutors during Quality Assurance Agency (QAA) visits of various kinds.

As a result of these activities the tutorial co-ordinator role has developed over time at LCC. It has growing status and recognition as part of the school management team, a heightened profile and liaison with all university services to students and student representatives and an increasing staff development role.

Relating to the wider aims of the university

This role is dependent on having management support which is best achieved by finding ways to harness institutional energy and resources. These will vary across context but are likely to include retention, lack of parity across the university (especially if identified by QAA audit) and managing a diverse student body or marketing strategy in relation to the National Student Survey (NSS). The last ten years have been a real opportunity for those of us concerned with academic support for students. Policy drivers have progressively covered retention, widening participation and the student experience, especially the first year experience. The NSS is the latest development.

However, all universities have private implicit aims as well as publicly espoused aims and it is important to be able to 'read' the institution to gain insight into these diverse aims and where institutional energy is focused. Within universities, different departments may have private aims that are quite at odds with the espoused and private aims of the university as a whole. This is likely to be affected by whether a department is a recruiter or selector of students. Later in this chapter we explore micropolitics as a theoretical lens for exploring these issues: one way of influencing the cultures of the university and department is by capturing the discourse.

To do this it is important to use discourse that the institution cannot reject. For example, subjects to address are:

- widening participation
- retention
- quality (particularly if an audit or review is imminent)
- student satisfaction (particularly if the university position in the NSS is a cause for concern)
- international students (particularly if recruitment or retention is an issue) and protection against litigation.

Harnessing resources

To return to the culture(s) operating amongst academic staff who actually populate the personal tutorial system, academic staff want to work in the best interests of their students. Few academics think that it is good for students to have less personal tutorial support. Resistance to the development of personal tutoring may come from concern over work intensification. Our model provides as much information as we can in as easily accessible a format as possible to support the role. More importantly, at LCC it is a priority for the tutorial co-ordinators group to fight for resources. This includes a time allowance formula for tutors which is based on the number of tutees and a time allowance for the tutorial co-ordinators to carry out their role. The group also exerts pressure to ensure that there is adequate and appropriate physical space for one-to-one personal tutorials, something that becomes increasing hard as space pressures militate against academic staff having their own rooms or even sharing with another person. These are standing items on our agenda and staff appreciate that we value and support this aspect of their job.

Strategic problems

Difficulties remain and we can't claim to have resolved all of them. We provide a time allowance for personal tutoring and the tutorial co-ordinators also have a time allowance for this. Increasingly, there is a problem with declining resources and concomitant pressures on staff in all aspects of academic life because of increasing student numbers, lack of physical space and increasing requirements for documentation of all processes. Within this pressurised environment, research continues to have more status than teaching and, within teaching, any kind of support activity has even less status in a way that is heavily gendered. Personal tutorial support is heavily dependent on the emotional labour of offering support and being caring (Morley, 1998), a role that often falls to women in the academy.

Academic staff may react by resisting monitoring and this resistance is becoming increasing sophisticated. It can take the form of cynical compliance to the letter but not to the spirit of the requirement, or simply doing nothing (Cowen, 1996). Also, whilst few academic staff are against personal tutorials *per se*, there are differing conceptions of learning: some believe that the role of higher education is to grow students and others who believe that higher education is a sorting mechanism to establish who is worthy of a degree. (Dore, 1997). This can affect what goes on *inside* a personal tutorial, an issue which is of growing concern.

But there are key strategies which include an emphasis on 'reading the university' to identify ways of tackling 'wicked issues' (Watson, 2000). These are such fundamental issues that the only way forward is to nibble round the edges, change what is changeable, in the hope that this will reduce the impact of the central problem. This has led us to a theoretical examination of what we are doing and why. We regard a theoretical understanding, particularly of complex underpinning issues, as a way of increasing our own knowledge and capacity to operate successfully within the academy in our project of developing personal tutoring. We have also realised that areas of student academic support gain respect and symbolic power with other academic staff if they are seen to be rooted in theory.

Conceptualising the personal tutorial strategy
The scholarship of student academic support

We have set our work in a context of scholarship of student academic support which covers, in addition to personal tutorial support, activities such as study support, language support, student to student mentoring, supplementary instruction and disability support. We regard these activities as sites for students to receive explicit introduction to, and dialogue on the expectations of higher education in the UK. Additionally, they create spaces which give us the opportunity to actually listen to the students so that institutional structural and cultural barriers are made visible as the first stage to challenge.

Student academic support is an underdeveloped area of the scholarship of teaching and learning. Many current theories of teaching and learning, including many approaches to learning, focus on the cognitive, to the exclusion of social factors (Haggis, 2002; Malcolm and Zukas, 2001). This is not to deny the usefulness of these models but they are only part of the picture. There is also a danger of the concept of the universal student or of sub-categories that are cognitive and hierarchical, and often binary, such as deep and surface approaches. Similarly, what the institution offers in terms of student academic support is often not recognised as part of the picture when teaching and learning is being considered.

We identify a strategic approach to tutoring within the following theoretical frameworks:

- We see personal tutorial systems as a way of building cultural capital (Bourdieu, 1997), particularly for students from backgrounds with little previous experience of UK higher education. We see cultural capital as what is valued by the educated elite of a particular culture at a particular point in history. Students arrive in higher education with different amounts of cultural capital that relate to their social background. One aspect that benefits from exploration is the hidden curriculum (Margolis, 2001), those tacit, unspoken rules and attitudes that manage to survive even the current 'tyranny of transparency' (Strathern, 2000). Students arrive in the *habitus* of their university with differing degrees of alignment with, and understanding of, institutional practices. This presents particular problems for students from socially disadvantaged backgrounds. For example, Archer *et al* (2003) explore the structural and cultural barriers faced by such students and Riddell *et al* (2005) view them from the perspective of another disadvantaged group, students with disabilities.

- We use the concept of 'the space between' (Ellsworth, 1997). In this construct, pedagogy is examined as an analogy with the film theory concept of 'mode of address', a particularly useful analogy and metaphor when working with academics in media disciplines. Ellsworth draws parallels between such questions as 'Who does this film think you are?', the relationship between the film's text and spectators' experience and interpretation and the pedagogic experience. She argues that unmediated dialogue is impossible, so uncritical reliance on ideas of transparency in communication with students is futile. This means that we need to be constantly aware of the assumptions we make about who we think our students are and how we tailor our pedagogic approaches to these assumptions. Also, as we have learned from complexity theory (Haggis, 2005), we need to look not only at the tutor and student but also at the characteristics of the interaction between them. This is always affected by both sides, experienced differently by both sides and cannot be fully controlled. Our experience indicates that this analysis not only gives insights into the tutor-student relationship but also helps when working with academic staff to build the personal tutoring project. Professional development is a teaching activity which requires us to think about who our audience actually is, and what assumptions we are making about their motivation and values.

■ We use the work of academic literacy theorists from both the UK and the US (Grimm, 1999; Lea and Street, 1998; Lillis, 2001). This focuses on academic writing as a social practice constructed both by wider social structures such as issues of class, ethnicity or gender and by the immediate institutional and disciplinary context, including rules and regulations, what is valued and the culturally specific nature of, for example, plagiarism. It gives us insights into contradictions in belief systems between staff and students (Higgins *et al*, 2002) and explores contradictory discourses and tensions with other subjectivities for both academics and students.

Micropolitics

To be successful in developing these ideas strategically within an institution we return to our earlier point about the need to read the department and university accurately. Our micropolitical perspective is based on the work of Hoyle (1982). Micropolitical strategies are located in 'the space between structures' (p88) where influence and alliances operate, and which represent multiple interests that go beyond the rational. They operate in spaces which are arenas for bargaining. They operate at the level of the personal, as material and symbolic gain and protection of territory and individual agency, at the level of the professional through commitment to particular forms of practice and of the political through commitment to particular political positions and values. The personal and political are often presented in the form of the professional, thus creating an illusion of rationality. Ball and Rowe (1991), in a similar vein, analyse organisations through perspectives of personal socio-political values, educational values and material interests.

Micropolitical perspectives examine 'strategies by which individuals and groups in organisational contexts seek to use their resources of power and influence to further their interests' (Hoyle, 1982 p88). Strategies are not fixed, can be long or short term and have multiple sources. They can be based on individual or group identities such as gender, position in hierarchy, subject discipline, professional interest or political views. Strategies used include control of rewards, controlling agendas, both formal and informal, and therefore deliberately 'losing' issues, secrecy around budgets and information and control over recruitment and training (thus 'cloning' to ensure that only those who fit in with the dominant power base are appointed). Control of the operation of rules and procedures, combined with distortion of information and denying outsiders competence, are other methods. Hoyle also suggests that strategies include 'losing' recommendations, 'rigging' agendas (both ways), 'massaging' the minutes, 'nobbling' individuals, 'inventing' consensus, 'interpreting' the opinions of outsiders and a receding locus of power so that we no longer can pinpoint who is actually making the decisions (Handy, 1976; Pettigrew, 1973, both quoted in Hoyle, 1982). This resonates with experiences in many universities of watching how key committees operate, how policy is developed, how information is distributed, how resources are allocated and how external agencies such as the QAA are quoted as reasons why something must happen.

To improve the position of personal tutoring within a university, it is important to invest time in analysing the university to identify formal and informal power relations at all levels, particularly in relation to control of resources and agenda setting. This involves identifying who actually makes the decisions – not an easy task in the contemporary academy. This should identify spaces for intervention in support of personal tutoring. There may be a current dominant discourse that can be used, such as the first year experience, or there may be new resources that can be harnessed such as the Centre for Excellence in Teaching and Learning (CETL). The strategy may be a formal paper to a committee, or it may be getting ten minutes to talk to the key person.

Conclusion

Over the years we have built our structures and practices on a particular model of personal tutoring which recognises universities as institutions which operate in a social system of cultural capital and complex, often tacit, institutional cultural assumptions. In this context we appreciate the complexity of the support relationship like any teaching relationship through an understanding of what is happening in 'the space between'. We use the personal tutorial space to explore these issues and elicit information that we can then use to affect university policy. We aim to affect these changes by capturing the discourse and being able to read the power relations of the institution so that we understand the context, culture and structures we are working within. We also use this space to explain to students the hidden power relations of institutional operations and the culturally specific nature of rules and regulations. Much of this is possible because we work as a group, who meet regularly and share experience and information from across the college. Our involvement includes input into professional development, including the Postgraduate Certificate in Learning and Teaching in Art and Design and school, college and university management and policy-making structures. What we have tried to do is pull together a research perspective on personal tutoring issues and practical implementation. Success in the latter depends on understanding the former.

From our theoretical perspective, our recommendations for those trying to develop personal tutoring include:

- identifying who are the powerful people in your context, what they are most anxious about and what language they talk. Is it student as customer, finance, status of the university, equal opportunities or teaching and learning?
- listening out for new money becoming available and assessing whether it can be accessed to support the development of personal tutoring.
- gathering a group – formal or informal – of others who are interested in personal tutoring and working out how to present your case in the dominant language. Identify whether presenting this case should involve trying to work your way up the hierarchy, speaking to particular individuals or delivering a formal paper to a committee or both.
- raising your profile as a group through asking to speak at as many other committees or groups as you can access. Have something specific to request which is in their power to give you or to help you to achieve.
- winning over personal tutors individually by offering them as much help and support as possible, particularly with difficult individual student issues and getting space and time to carry out the personal tutoring role successfully.
- at the first opportunity, arguing for a middle management layer to manage personal tutoring. Be modest in the resources you initially request but ensure that those in this new role meet regularly as a group to support each other and share good practice.

By using strategies like these we have some chance of achieving university recognition of the importance and potential of personal tutorial systems and of ensuring greater success with espoused government policies such as widening participation and student retention. More importantly, we are making a contribution to student success within a wider framework of equity and social justice.

Section 3
Issues and implications for staff

11

Changing practice in tutorial provision within post-compulsory education

Sally Wootton

Introduction

This chapter is intended for educators who are responsible for managing tutoring provision or for undertaking a personal tutoring role, and is relevant in a further and higher education context. The aim is to bring lucidity to the personal tutoring role, proposing areas of common purpose that may be shared by the tutoring community. The argument for change concentrates on a proposal for the repositioning of personal tutoring, making it central to the learning experience. This proposal is based on the importance placed by students on the tutorial relationship and the demands created by a greater complexity of the needs of an increasingly diverse cohort.

We can all find ourselves in situations where we think we understand what is expected of us and assume that others are confident about what they are doing. When we talk to colleagues we realise that many of us are suffering similar apprehensions and misunderstandings. This is true of the personal tutoring role. Because the nature of the work has not been clearly defined, the confusion of tutors results in a variety of misguided historical practices.

These misconceptions remain through lack of policy that would otherwise elucidate the rationale and central themes for tutoring provision. Personal tutoring is often regarded as part of broader student service guidelines or curriculum entitlement. Reference is rarely made to integrating a holistic approach to learners' development or differentiating provision to meet a diverse range of learners' needs. The lack of detail can result in disparate provision across the institution which leads to student dissatisfaction. It also creates unnecessary anxiety for tutors who are concerned about their own performance which they cannot evaluate due to lack of clarity about the purpose and content of the role.

This research serves two purposes: it reveals students' needs for and expectations of personal tutoring as well as personal tutors' shared understanding of its purpose and content. It explores the professional skills and expertise required to meet the demands of the tutoring role competently.

Advocating a need for change in tutorial provision

The Government agenda to widen participation in higher education has led to an increasingly complex cohort. Allied to this is a responsibility for each institution to offer appropriate, differentiated tutorial provision to meet the specific needs of non-traditional minority groups entering post-compulsory education. Widening participation has encouraged an increase in new learners who may be the first in their family to attend college or university. They often bring a range of anxieties relating to family attitude, lack of personal support, low self-esteem or negative peer pressure. They may also contend with a combination of worries relating to financial, welfare or academic difficulties.

Having successfully recruited learners, traditional or otherwise, a duty is placed on the institution to ensure adequate measures to support them in their endeavours towards academic achievement, professional development and personal growth. Examples of minority groups entering as a result of widening participation policies include:

- early college transfer students (14 to 16 years-old) who opt out of their final year at school and undertake vocational study in a post-compulsory institution. These students have often displayed behaviours or attitudes that schools have found difficult to manage
- care leavers who face a variety of personal circumstances that can impact on their ability to engage in or maintain post-compulsory education. Some may have missed much of their compulsory education through moves to different foster homes and require additional learning support to help them with their studies
- asylum seekers and refugees who experience a broad range of personal and welfare barriers to study. Difficulties can range from not having a known date of birth, which restricts their ability to enrol for study, to a fear of institutions and giving confidential information

- adult learners, often anxious about returning to study, can carry added pressures of family responsibilities and in some cases conflict with partners related to their decision to study

- students entering higher education through non-traditional routes such as advanced modern apprenticeships or vocational qualifications.

These examples offer some indication of the diversity that currently exists and the sensitive nature of personal tutoring.

The impact of increased diversity on provision is far-reaching. Personal tutors are charged with supporting more students with a broader range of issues. In practice this means greater demand on personal tutors' time spent providing extensive one-to-one support for increasingly complex issues. This has led to an indistinguishable boundary between tutoring and counselling, leaving many personal tutors feeling increasingly responsible for their students' welfare and unsure of referral timings.

This broadening of the personal tutoring role is compounded by the wider demands for recording students' personal and professional development. This changes the shape of tutoring, demanding a more structured approach to group tutoring than was previously considered necessary. The require-ment for measurable outcomes, whereas previously tutoring was a informal exchange, has created tension and confusion about its agreed purpose. When Ofsted and QAA insist on quantifying the success of personal tutoring, they look at retention and achievement statistics. Paradoxically, this frustrates the independent nature of advice that should be offered through personal tutoring. For example, when the best course of action for a student may be to transfer to a different course or leave their studies part-way through to accept a job offer (which is often why students do not return to study following work placement), this would be seen as a failure because the student did not com-plete. There is no method of acknowledging that learning has taken place up to that point and may well have been instrumental in giving the student con-fidence to make the decision. There is also an assumption by regulatory bodies that evidence of learning can only be judged by the group tutoring schemes of work, which works against the flexibility required to address the developmental needs of students as they face new challenges.

Creating a shared understanding of the purpose and content of tutoring should enable us to defend our policy and activities in relation to regulatory requirements. A good starting point would be to acknowledge how the personal tutor role has changed, which lies in the recognition that in practice it has become central to the learning experience as opposed to additional to core learning. In acknowledging this we can be more confident in developing institutional policy, clearly setting out the personal tutoring ethos, the institution's commitment to it, how differentiation is supported and how personal tutoring underpins the holistic learning experience.

Defining the purpose of tutorial provision

Cantor *et al* (1995) acknowledge a growing recognition of the importance of student support services in improving retention and achievement. They also allude to the need for support services to take account of the diverse groups of students engaged in post-compulsory education. Student support services encompasses a multitude of activities including counselling, careers advice, finance and welfare. Personal tutoring is a core activity, linking student services and curriculum support to the student. The personal tutor acts as a conduit between the student and the institution, and is responsible for supporting the student in their personal, professional and academic development. The personal tutor is therefore a key player in both the students' achievement and progression and the institution's success.

Tutoring, according to Wheeler and Birtle (1993) is primarily aimed at facilitating students' personal development, monitoring progress and providing a link between the student and the institution. They propose that in order to achieve these aims personal tutors should act as both confidante and advocate on the students' behalf. Other contributors to the development of post-compulsory tutoring, such as Lublin (1997) and Lago and Shipton (1994), share this position but also refer to the role as supporting students through periods of transition. Although these are useful definitions my research observes tutors' needs for the complexity of the role to be made more explicit and acknowledged.

Research methodology

This research has been undertaken using a critical theorist approach, ensuring a collaborative approach at all stages. To this end, the participants were chosen on the basis that were either a recipient of tutoring or a provider of tutoring, so that they could relate concrete experience and offer interpretation to inform the study.

The empirical research was undertaken in two phases at two institutions in the Yorkshire and Humber region. Each institution provides a broad range of further and higher education programmes across several campuses. The participating institutions are situated in similar economic areas, both recovering from the decline of the coalmining industry, and are seeking to address the skills needs of the local population. Progression to full time education at 16 is below national average in both districts.

The student cohorts drawn from the two institutions differed in their level of study. In the first phase a questionnaire was circulated to 300 higher education students at the end of the academic year. This ensured that the respondents in Year 1 had experienced sufficient personal tutoring to enable them to comment on the provision and its effect on learning. In total 67 responses were received, as shown below.

Figure 1: Pattern of Higher Education Student Respondents

Current Year Of Study	1st Year	2nd Year	3rd Year	No data
	46.3%	44.8%	3.5%	3.4%
Attendance	Full time	Part Time	Distance	
	92.5%	5%	0%	
Age Group	16-20	21+		
	68.7%	31.3%		
Gender	Male	Female	No data	
	35.8%	61.2%	3%	

During the second phase, the questionnaire was accessed by further education students in hard copy and via the student intranet. In total there were 73 respondents, as shown below.

Figure 2: Pattern of Further Education Student Respondents

Current Year Of Study	1st Year	2nd Year	3rd Year	No data
	68%	18.5%	11%	3%
Attendance	Full time	Part Time	Distance	
	93%	3%	4%	
Age Group	16-20	21+		
	99%	1%		
Gender	Male	Female	No data	
	33%	47%	20%	

This offered comparable perceptions of provision between the two levels of study as well as between student and tutor. The majority of tutors in each institution were involved in teaching on both further and higher education programmes. It is interesting that there were no significant differences in tutors' attitudes between the two cohorts, referring to students *per se* and not separating the level of study for their own purposes. Significant findings were found between further and higher education students' perceptions of the purpose and content of tutoring, some of which are highlighted in this chapter.

The preliminary questionnaires were used to engage with potential student respondents who might later take part in focus groups. At the same time initial data was gathered as a starting point for the inductive exploration. Tutors were engaged as part of the institution's tutor development programme. Focus groups were carried out which separated students and tutors to gather qualitative data which related to their experiences. In the focus groups methods included brainstorming activities using magna boards, freestyle drawing and discussion. Both students and tutors described critical incidents: the data was translated into written narrative.

The rationale for these methods was to gather data from which themes would emerge in the spirit of grounded theory (Strauss and Corbin, 1997) to provide a fresh view of the subject matter as it appears today. Allowing the data to 'speak to me' in this way revealed emergent themes. In analysing the data, personal tutor typologies were explored to further professional development. Findings relating to the purpose and content of tutoring were used to inform policy and procedure so that 'the research can, by intervention, engage in a social process of change management' (Garvey and Williamson, 2002). Being able to examine the research data meant that they could be evaluated by the participants.

Research findings

The exploration of students' needs found that students describe personal tutoring as planning for self-improvement. They saw this as an overarching reason for the interaction, encompassing both academic development and pastoral care, including understanding and addressing a range of students' anxieties.

It was found that students are uncertain about their academic performance. One student described the beginning of the course as 'a steep learning curve' and commented that he and a number of fellow students 'felt like packing it in' because of worries about the amount of assessment work required and 'everything being new'. They were lonely: one student commented 'You haven't got the support there to cope with it'. Others agreed that the amount of work was a worry, as was its nature: presentations and academic writing. This was compounded by apprehension about tutor expectations of the level of work produced, which varied considerably between tutors. The main areas concerning students entering higher education in relation to academic support were:

- essay writing
- report writing
- presentation skills
- organisational skills
- spelling and grammar

These findings indicate a need to prepare and equip students with the tools to enable them to achieve in their studies. This supports the current government's agenda to improve basic skills and integrate key skills in schools and further education. It is evident that some students still lack confidence in these basic academic skills which are required to cope successfully with their assessments: their absence can lead to early disengagement. This gives greater emphasis to the need for early recognition and intervention for students requiring additional study support. The significance of personal tutoring lies in ensuring tutors have the time and the skills to enable them to recognise when students require study support and to encourage disclosure so that students with individual learning needs, such as support for dyslexia, gain access to these services. In addition to being prepared for the academic rigours of the course, there is also an expectation to recognise and evidence employability skills through curriculum and professional development activities.

Group tutorial

The are problems in encouraging some students to attend group tutorial. The research found that a strong body of students thought that 'the time could be better spent working on assignments' as they felt no clear purpose was given to the sessions. Explicit purpose enables the tutor to plan appropriately to ensure that the time spent is contributing to the students' development, and that the student sees the value in attending. These are some of the students' responses when asked about what the purpose of group tutoring should be:

- Group bonding and socialising: An opportunity to meet with other students and get to know them. This was a social, relaxed activity and refers back to anxieties expressed about not having support to help them cope.

- Receiving information about College: This includes information about college-wide student forums, activities and services, as well as the course module and assessment information.

- Group discussion and problem solving: Focuses on teamwork and sharing ideas for problem-solving, talking things over as a group and gaining support from knowing how others feel.

- Discussing the course and progression: Discussion about course content, difficulties with particular subject areas and a focus on progression after the course such as applying to enter higher education or planning their first career move.

- Learning and development: This area refers to an enjoyment of learning as an activity and learning new skills to prepare for the future and for independent living.

- Engaging with the tutor: This became a strong theme emerging throughout the research and relates to tutors having time to engage and foster a good student/tutor relationship.

- Classroom environment: This reflected different views ranging from having an opportunity for peace and quiet, the sessions being more laid back, to it being fun and active. It was suggested that the environment should be in keeping with the activity.

These aspects encompassed a sharing of information, being able to discuss issues, complaints and the opportunity for group learning, all of which they valued to support their personal and academic development. The range of expectations that emerged were shared by further and higher education students. Further education students expanded on this by expressing a need to prepare for independent living by addressing financial management, understanding the work environment and exploring opportunities for progression into higher education.

All students made it clear that there are significant differences in their needs as they progress through their studies. In the first year they require support in settling into college or university and there should be a focus on study skills to enable them to approach their assessment work confidently. There should also be a forum for group bonding and socialising where an empathetic support network can be created. In the second year they want to focus on career planning and preparation for progression, which was inappropriate for the first year and too late for the second year.

In discussion, the tutors agreed with the students but there was interesting discussion about who owns the agenda in tutoring sessions. Whereas tutors saw group tutorial as predominantly a didactic session of delivery, students proposed a joint agenda where both parties brought topics for discussion to be agreed through negotiation. Carl Rogers (1983) spoke of how classrooms became more exciting places as he learned to trust his students. Allowing himself to loosen his grip on controlling the sessions facilitated his students in 'blossoming out as growing human beings' (1983). If we acknowledge that the purpose of personal tutoring is to facilitate holistic personal as well as academic development, there is value in the students' proposal for a flexible, shared agenda.

Individual Tutoring
Students propose that individual tutoring should be relevant to their needs and that, as with group tutoring, both the tutor and student should be able to take their individual agendas to tutorial meetings for discussion, implying a negotiated process similar to that of a mentoring relationship. Their views of the purpose of individual tutoring are:

- Personal support: Includes an opportunity to have confidential discussion about welfare and other personal issues that may negatively affect learners' progress and/or achievement and explore strategies for dealing with issues. It is also seen as an opportunity for learners to put their own views across and receive one-to-one feedback.
- Academic support: This includes study skills, managing workload, work experience and career development. The opportunity to discuss assignments and review professional development and academic progress.
- Attitudinal aspects: This third aspect relates to the accessibility and attitude of the tutor and the physical environment in which personal tutoring takes place.

The third theme, attitudinal aspects, is complex. It highlights the significance of the tutor/student relationship to the learning experience and goes on to explore the skills and attributes required for effective tutoring.

Issues in planning and implementing tutorial provision
This research has found that planning for tutoring provision is often seen as a secondary exercise which only happens when course modules have been timetabled. The allocation of personal tutors is often linked with being a course co-ordinator. This can create tensions between the two roles when the personal tutor is needed to act as an advocate for a student, particularly in

disciplinary cases. When the course co-ordinator is not the personal tutor for that group the personal tutor is allocated on the basis of tutor availability. This approach, which may be common across the sector, takes no account of whether individual tutors possess the skills, qualities or expertise required to carry out the tutoring role effectively.

Consultation with tutors has shown that some tutors would prefer to opt out of the personal tutoring role. They explain that they entered teaching to teach their subject specialism and are not comfortable with the additional respon-sibility of counselling or mothering. Insisting that they undertake personal tutoring may develop attitudes towards the role that reveal a lack of genuine engagement with students. Conversely, some tutors who like personal tutor-ing can be possessive over the support they offer and avoid involving third parties. They behave as though they own their tutor group and are sensitive about retention and achievement figures when students leave or transfer courses. They voice their dislike of interference by other parties with 'their' students' development. This is as detrimental to students as a neglectful tutoring relationship, because it obstructs access to areas of expertise a student needs or other professionals who could be helpful.

Summary

This chapter has considered the shape of personal tutoring today against the backdrop of changes in post-compulsory education. We have seen how the emphasis on tutoring as a contribution to improving retention and achieve-ment is not clearly reflected in approaches to design and implementation. The importance of reflecting the tutoring ethos in the institution's mission statement and tutoring policy has been discussed and the need to demon-strate a cohesive approach to academic and personal development and student support has been highlighted. Having explored students' perceptions of tutoring it is possible to offer a concise overview of what students seek from both group and individual tutoring, enabling provision to be designed with purpose and clarity. The framework provided here can be confidently imple-mented on the basis that students and tutors share the same perceptions, and this reduces the disparity between expectations and provision.

We have also explored how increased diversity in the student population places a greater burden on the personal tutor providing individual support. There has been an increase in demand for tutors' time as more students are considered to be at risk. In attempting to alleviate the tutors' burden, a second level of intervention can often be effective in supporting the student. Mentoring relationships in education may be used as a means to support students with low self-esteem, low aspirations or lack of motivation, (Crowther and Wootton, 2002). Mentoring provides an informal, confidential forum for students to discuss their issues and develop their own coping strategies and is often preferable to the student who feels they need one-to-one support but do not think that counselling is appropriate.

During this research a number of practitioners have proposed that the way forward is to bring the tutoring role into line with other professional occupations such as mentoring, coaching and counselling. These professional communities work to given standards and competences and are acknowledged as offering specific skills and expertise. For this to occur, at least on an institutional level, it is necessary to ensure that personal tutors have the basic skills to perform the role effectively. It is useful to make the desirable skills and qualities explicit in a personnel specification allied to a role description. This approach offers a comprehensible direction for tutors and enables individual continuing professional development (CPD) to be identified in a bid to create highly skilled practitioners in this essential area of work.

12

'Who's looking after me?'
– Supporting new personal tutors

Pauline Ridley

Introduction

This chapter describes attempts to improve the support available to personal tutors at the University of Brighton. The title is from a typical comment from one new lecturer: 'I'm trying to look after all these students with all their problems – but who's looking after me? '

The focus of this chapter is on the perceptions, experience and well being of tutors rather than those of the students, though the two are necessarily connected. The developments described have emerged from work with new and experienced academic staff undertaken by the University Centre for Learning and Teaching over a number of years. This was not originally framed as a research project; accordingly the material presented is drawn from a variety of sources:

- informal discussions with several cohorts of new lecturers undertaking the University's Postgraduate Certificate in Learning and Teaching in Higher Education
- written reflections (for which permission to quote brief extracts was given retrospectively) recorded in response to a study pack on personal tutoring used in that course
- qualitative research (Barlow and Antoniou, 2003) into the experiences of new lecturers at the university
- discussions with new and experienced academics in a variety of other contexts, including staff development sessions and a working group on personal tutoring

■ an email survey of personal tutors across the university. Most of those
who responded were experienced staff and their participation usually reflected a particular interest in tutoring. Their responses are not necessarily typical, but provided a helpful comparison to those of new tutors
and some important additional insights.

The University of Brighton context

Brighton is a post-1992 university with campuses in and around Brighton and
Eastbourne and specialist centres in Hastings and Tunbridge Wells. It has a
strong emphasis on professional and vocational education and research.
There are just over 21,000 students, of whom around 58 per cent are full time
undergraduates, with around 6 per cent taught in partner colleges. Echoing
the national picture, around 6.5 per cent declare a disability. Data on widening participation shows that retention, progression and achievement
statistics for students with non-standard entry qualifications are similar to
those of their peers.

The University has been regularly commended by external examiners, QAA
institutional audits and subject reviews for the quality of student support and
guidance provided. Most academic staff take pastoral support seriously and
several have undertaken research into this aspect of the student experience
(Challenger-Gillett, 2005; Sosabowski *et al*, 2003; Wilcox *et al*, 2005).

In 1995 the University introduced a personal tutoring policy, entitling each
student to have a member of staff regularly available to offer personal tutoring support. The policy does not prescribe a uniform tutorial system but ack-
nowledges the range of central and course-based support which had evolved
to suit different disciplinary and professional contexts.

The policy also includes entitlements for tutors, in particular to have access
to training and to a school liaison tutor, who can act as a further source of
support and advice and as a link between the school and student services and
other support systems within the University.

New lecturers' experience of tutoring

Increasing student numbers have meant that in some schools new lecturers
may be asked to take on personal tutor responsibilities soon after arriving at
the university. How does their experience match the principles embedded in
the policy?

Lecturers appointed to the university with less than two years experience of
teaching are encouraged to undertake the Postgraduate Certificate in Learn-

ing and Teaching in Higher Education. Over the course of an academic year they attend workshop sessions and engage independently with study packs on different topics, building up a portfolio of evidence and reflection about their teaching.

Participation in action learning sets, composed of around six colleagues from different schools, is an important element of the course (McGill and Beaty, 1995). These meetings provide members with regular structured peer support for their teaching and a safe space for them to explore detailed queries and concerns. A recurrent theme for many new academics, whether or not they have formal tutorial responsibilities, is anxiety about the level, as they perceive it, of students' support needs and fears that they may be unable to fulfil them.

Anecdotal evidence from set meetings is echoed in the findings from a series of qualitative interviews into the experience of new lecturers at the University:

> [New lecturers] were often overwhelmed by students' need for support. They ...perceived students as too dependent and demanding and, at times, inconsiderate. [They] felt that too little time was allowed for pastoral support and personal tutoring (Barlow and Antoniou, 2003)

To some extent this is a realistic response to new lecturers' actual experiences with students. But it also reflects a pervasive discourse of student neediness, found in much of the media representations of higher education and in the language often used, unconsciously, by some academics to refer to students.

Despite the fact that developments, such as the Special Educational Needs and Disability Act 2001, and various widening participation initiatives, are welcomed by the majority of academic staff, in practice as well as in principle, the language of support needs and entitlements which they may engender has helped to fuel this discourse. A minority of staff consider that widening participation means dumbing down, although retention, progression and achievement statistics for students with non-standard entry qualifications are equal to those of their peers at Brighton, playing into a stereotype of the contemporary student demanding more academic or pastoral support than in the past, when the tutors themselves were students.

These views may be expressed disparagingly: 'students nowadays expect to be spoon-fed' or sympathetically, 'they need to do so much more outside work than when we were students, they need all the help we can give ...' , but

129

they share a common image of the academic tutor as parent, with the students as troubled or troublesome children.

Maternal metaphors and images of clingy children are prevalent, sometimes expressed in a despairing tone, sometimes resentfully:

> They [students] lack confidence ... I find them quite clingy, sometimes I feel like a mother with about, you know, a hundred babies hanging off ... (New lecturer, quoted in Barlow and Antoniou, 2003)

Another lecturer used the term 'Cling-ons', half-humorously, half in exasperation, to describe the many students who turned up unannounced at her office, constantly seeking advice and support. However, she had set no limits on her availability and was genuinely taken aback by the suggestion that she should introduce a signing-up system or confine open door times to a single day a week. Unlimited access, followed by resentment when students take advantage of this, is a surprisingly common pattern among new academics.

I return below to the possible causes of the inability to set boundaries – but it is worth remembering that it takes place in a context of increasing workloads for all university staff. A workload survey undertaken by the lecturers' union NATFHE found that 69 per cent of respondents worked an average of eleven unpaid hours a week.

> .. lecturers repeatedly told how they routinely sacrifice evenings and weekends to try and keep up with their work..... 'It leads to a constant feeling of strain and exploitation, especially as the feeling is always that we should be doing more'. (NATFHE, 2005)

This is echoed in many course participants' reflective journals:

> ... constant phone interruptions, tutees taking up time, dealing with e-mails

> I was all fired up yesterday morning to start working [...] then I opened my diary and I wanted to cry. Where exactly is the time?

Brighton is certainly not unusual in this respect, in conditions of work or the nature of the students, and most new lecturers find it easier to manage their time as they gain experience. Nevertheless, such accounts raise the question of why academic staff who are feeling so overstretched can find it hard to say no, even when they recognise that what they see as excessive demands from their students.

Part of the problem appears to be the absence of a secure sense of what it means to be an effective personal tutor. Most new lecturers have a choice of models for other aspects of their work. As students they are likely to have experienced all kinds of approaches to lecturing, seminars and other activities; as new lecturers they will usually have opportunities to sit in on colleagues' classes. With or without formal training they bring to their own early teaching a basic idea of what is expected and the reassuring knowledge that there are many different ways to fulfil the role and that most students will survive and forgive less than perfect teaching.

Few academics have equivalent breadth of experience of tutoring. As undergraduates they will normally have had a single personal tutor, at most followed by some postgraduate supervision. It is also unlikely that they will have had opportunities to sit in on colleagues' personal tutorials.

> In my role of personal tutor I had to see a few students last year but felt very uncomfortable in these sessions as I wasn't happy with what exactly my role was, having never been on the receiving end myself as a student. I just got through the meetings! (New lecturer journal)

They themselves may have endured inadequate tutorial supervision:

> It... was not a very positive experience for me. I didn't particularly relate to the tutor and he didn't really know who I was. He was given a list of names of students... and told he had to see us every so often. He didn't want to do it and we didn't want to be there.

> My tutor was a professor, we always used surnames... It was a very stark divide between lowly student and academic staff. With hindsight he was there for his research, not to teach, and was not very good at it either and gave me no support or help, but this was the normal culture there.

> My only recollection is of a glass of sherry one December.....

> (Responses to email survey)

When new lecturers talk about tutors who were never there for me – I was just left to struggle, they are emphatic that they do not want to be like that themselves. However, if there is a shortage of positive real life models, this leaves space to fantasise what it means to be a good tutor. Setting unrealistic targets can then generate conflicting feelings:

> I've put a sign on my door saying... do not disturb, I am working, but they still come and knock on the door and open it and you know... and then people say, well just lock it and ... kind of things which I've never wanted to have been .. from being a student... (New lecturer, in Barlow and Antoniou, 2003)

Awkwardness of expression reflects these difficult feelings. Notice also that when colleagues pass on more cynical coping mechanisms such as ('just lock the door'), younger tutors are still close enough to their own student days to identify with what it feels like to be on the receiving end of this approach and to reject it as a strategy.

In contrast, experienced staff are much more relaxed about setting boundaries to suit their own ways of working but know how to recognise and respond to a genuine crisis when necessary:

> I will always respond to emails ASAP but in many cases will offer temporary help or solutions until I can arrange a time to see them. Once these rules are agreed I don't find students have too much difficulty working within them. In an emergency my colleagues will see one of my students and *vice-versa*.
>
> I have no problem giving my tutees my mobile number. My one rule is that they don't call or text before 8am or after 9pm. It seems to work really well and only on one occasion when something pretty bad was happening to one of my tutees did I get a call at midnight. In this case I was happy to take the call. I would rather they feel they can contact me and get it all off their chest than bottle it up and let it impact negatively on their studies.
>
> I encourage them to text me when there are specific issues ... I find this works quite effectively as a filter, students tend only to text important information and it provides an indirect point of contact
>
> [Students] always seem willing to come back if it is not really urgent. Similarly, I think that if it is urgent I have a moral obligation to see them straightaway
>
> (Responses to email survey, 2005)

Experienced tutors also know that it is often better to trouble shoot early before it gets bigger and that time spent tutoring early on in a process can save time later down the line. For new staff the difficulty is in developing the professional sixth sense that enables them to distinguish between urgent and non-urgent situations and – just as importantly, in articulating ground rules with sufficient confidence that students will respect these limits.

Improving the support for new tutors

The university introduced a system of departmental liaison tutors as part of its personal tutoring policy. The intention was to provide a point of contact between academic schools and student services and to ensure that a senior member of staff was available to advise other tutors on issues such as referrals. In many schools, the system still works well but over time the liaison tutor network has met less frequently. Busy timetables and changes of staff have also tended to erode a shared understanding of their role in supporting newly appointed tutors.

A working group convened in 2003-4 to review personal tutoring re-endorsed the policy but found that better guidance and support for personal tutors was needed. In response to this and to the experiences being reported by new lecturers, the Centre for Learning and Teaching developed a study pack on personal tutoring for use in the Postgraduate Certificate. The following year this was adapted as a more general guide, which is now updated annually and circulated to all tutors through school offices. It is also available online at http://staffcentral.brighton.ac.uk/clt/resources/personal_tutor.htm, along with other resources such as case studies, intended as a starting point for departmental discussion of tutoring issues.

Despite differences of tone and emphasis, the guide has retained many of the prompts to reflection that formed the basis of the original study pack. The reason is that a key element of previous face to face work with new tutors has been to help them acknowledge and manage their emotional responses to the role. Over the past few years it has become clear that rather than just being told, through policy statements and other general advice, what tutors should do, they need encouragement to articulate and explore their own expectations and anxieties. Crucially they need reassurance that it is better to be a good enough tutor than to aim for an unrealistic ideal.

> low self esteem and high expectations .. [lead] to bouts of fear and despair ... setting expectations which are too high and not achieving them can be disappointing. (New lecturer journal)

The phrase 'good enough' is of course a reference to the work of Donald Winnicott, the British psychoanalyst whose writings, and this term in particular, are now widely cited in a variety of therapeutic and non-therapeutic contexts. We do not necessarily make this connection explicit, since some lecturers may be uncomfortable with the intrusion of psychoanalytic theory into discussions of their academic role, but Winnicott's concept of the 'good-enough' parent has particular relevance to tutorial relationships and to the concerns discussed above.

> The good-enough mother ... starts off with an almost complete adaptation to her infant's needs, and as time proceeds she adapts less and less completely, gradually, according to the infant's growing ability to deal with her failure ... (Winnicott, 1965)

Similarly, one of the most valuable insights for new personal tutors is that their task is not to provide the solutions to all their students' problems but to help build students' independence and their capacity to help themselves. To recognise this and put it into practice requires clarity about their own responses to the role.

Early in the guide, we ask tutors to think back to their own experiences as students and the different kinds of pastoral and academic support they received. This elicits some powerful memories, such as those quoted above, of absent or unhelpful tutors. However, many new and experienced staff also report the existence of a key individual who made a difference, or helped them through difficult patches. Sometimes the contrast is sharp:

> My first tutor was always too busy to give me any encouragement or anything at all, come to think about it. ... She was possibly the last member of staff I would have wanted to go to with any personal/study problems. She was very sarcastic and offhand in her comments to all students, not just to me and never knew anyone's names..... The second tutor bought patience, accessibility, understanding, willingness to give help/advise outside of direct sphere and to some extent a level of friendship and trust. [He] was always available for a chat, even if it meant coming back the next day, gave me answers when I asked questions and would offer help by email. I never felt intimidated or belittled, or that I was an inconvenience, but that he wanted to get the very best out of me academically. (Email survey, 2005)

Tutors need to consider how such experiences, negative and positive, may have influenced their own approach.

> .... knowing that there was somebody there who gave a damn. I'll never forget my tutor phoning me one morning ... asking me why I hadn't submitted an assignment and whether there were any circumstances I would like to have taken into consideration. You got a real sense that [they] cared (which is I something I make sure I reflect in my role now). (Email survey)

Some remember their own independence but acknowledge the need to be flexible:

> [My tutor was] very remote, students kept at a distance (old university style) left to yourself to sort things out – stand on your own feet!... For me [this] was not a problem but for students requiring support a more personal and friendly approach was needed. (Email survey)

The key point for new tutors is to recognise that there is no single correct approach. Instead, awareness of their own preferred tutoring style is helpful, especially where this might conflict with other expectations or the demands of a particular situation.

> My preferred [tutoring] style is that of a mentor but in my short time of being a tutor I have had to adapt to many various situations where I have to adopt the role of a parent, supervisor and counsellor. Also I have soon come to

realise that a lot of my tutorial time is spent progress chasing. (New lecturer journal)

Personal tutors must be aware of the university policy on student entitlements and how this is implemented locally. The intention is not to monitor compliance with institutional policy but to provide openings for discussion. So we encourage them to ask colleagues about this to recognise that there may be variation between written guidelines and what actually happens in practice and to raise any queries with their school liaison tutor or other senior colleague. There is also a brief explanation of the framework for personal development planning (PDP) currently being introduced across the university to draw together the range of existing PDP initiatives to encourage greater student autonomy and bring purpose and clarity to scheduled progress reviews.

The guide contains basic advice on such issues as setting up and managing tutorial meetings. Common student problems are outlined along with potential sources of help, contact details and emergency numbers for specialist services. Some sections were drawn up in conjunction with the University counselling service and emphasise the need to know when to refer students for specialist assistance, rather than offering well-meaning but amateur advice.

The desirability of establishing clear boundaries for the tutorial role is stressed throughout. Tutors are invited to consider their own preconceptions about accessibility and offered various suggestions to help keep the workload more manageable, for instance by establishing peer support groups or holding occasional group tutorials to deal with common academic issues.

Comments such as 'I felt fully prepared and in control' and 'This ... has given me more confidence in my role' suggest that establishing more realistic roles for themselves as good enough tutors can allay initial anxieties about controlling demand.

Widening the support network

The guide has received positive feedback but it can never be more than a starting point. Tutors' confidence and skills develop most rapidly when induction and written guidelines are supplemented by continuing peer support within their own department:

> The ... guidelines ... [were] particularly helpful and enlightening.. and assistance from [liaison tutor] and more experienced colleagues is always available. I think my own effectiveness as a personal tutor ...is supported by a good tutorial system (New lecturer journal)

> I find more experienced colleagues to be very helpful, informative and open to giving advice ... a bit like a personal tutors' tutor if you like. (Email survey)

Almost every experienced tutor who responded to the survey also referred to the importance of informal support networks. Typical comments included:

> Our team has a very supportive way of working and if there are difficulties I can go to other members for support.

> [I have] a great bunch of experienced and sensible colleagues who are always happy to help.

> My office mate and colleagues ... are all very supportive.

> We talk as a course team about how to deal with difficult situations.

> Everyone in the department is there to support each other (amazing but true) so I never feel that I have to deal with a problem alone.

Surprisingly the support needs of new tutors parallel those of new undergraduates, with a close-knit fabric of different forms of support being preferable to any single solution.

If so, this suggests that at induction tutors should receive basic information and guidance, preferably within a supportive environment such as that offered by the postgraduate certificate action learning sets. Then, just as most students benefit from the one-to-one relationship with a personal tutor – 'someone who gives a damn' – to help them grow into independence, so most tutors also appreciate the existence of a senior colleague or mentor, such as the liaison tutor, to provide advice and reassurance and a point of contact with specialist services.

But just as Wilcox *et al* (2005) have shown that social networks play a vital role in the first year undergraduate experience, so universities need to encourage the informal collegiate networks so valued by tutors – and to ensure that new staff are included in them. Properly supported, most staff discover that tutoring is not a source of additional stress but a rewarding and valuable part of being an academic.

> [I] wouldn't give it up. One part of the job where it is possible to make a difference to someone.

> I really enjoy it. I like the personal relationships that I am able to build up with students and am still in contact with a great number of my ex-students ... I also like seeing people develop and overcoming problems to go on and achieve great things. (Email survey)

In a mass higher education system that kind of job satisfaction is worth preserving.

13

Issues for online personal tutoring: Staff perceptions from an online distance learning programme

Rosalind Crouch and Ruth Barrett

Introduction

Personal tutoring is considered important and necessary for online and distance learning students (QAA, 2004). Online students can feel lonely and isolated (Paulsen, 1998) and communication and support from staff is greatly valued (Rekkedal, 1997). However, for staff used to on-campus personal tutoring, online personal tutoring can present challenges as well as some benefits. We report on a study of a new online Masters programme in Computer Science, looking at staff experiences of the advantages and disadvantages of personal tutoring entirely online, as compared with their previous experiences on-campus. Staff liked certain aspects, such as responding to and initiating communication more at their own pace but generally found the lack of face-to-face communication caused them difficulties with personal tutoring, due to more limited channels of feedback and a greater difficulty in clarifying meaning. They also found online personal tutoring time-consuming. We make recommendations at the end of the chapter for partially overcoming some of these difficulties, such as the availability of additional communication channels and verbal and non-verbal strategies for computer-mediated communication. We also consider issues of support and training for online personal tutors.

Background

We wanted to find out how effectively staff thought they could build relationships with students online and whether students could achieve a sense of belonging on the course. We also wanted to find out how effectively staff thought they could deal with student personal and study problems entirely online and how they experienced using email as the main channel of communication for individual personal tutoring.

We defined personal tutoring as involving building a sense of student belonging and establishing relationships and dealing with student problems and issues. We have followed Crouch *et al* (1998) in categorising student problems brought to us as study or personal problems. Crouch's study found that academic performance improved over the year for on-campus computer science students with both categories of problem. Also that those without apparent problems, who attended scheduled meetings with their personal tutor, compared well to students who did not attend. Similar improvements in performance and retention were found with an experimental group of distance computer science students who were given personalised attention by a personal tutor (Rekkedal, 1991).

Structured interviews were conducted with online staff, whose previous experience was of on-campus student support and personal tutoring. These took place after the first year of operation of a three year part time Masters programme in Computer Science where all interaction and assessment is online and student numbers are as yet fairly small. The programme begins with an induction period, followed by a number of 13 week courses running consecutively. The promotion of staff/student and student/student interaction is considered important throughout the programme, and is initiated in the induction process, subsequently following Salmon's 5-stage model (Salmon, 2004).

Although students have the flexibility to choose when and where they study, they are constrained by the assessment due every thirteenth week. An inability to complete this assessment can bring study and personal problems to a tutor's attention if these have not been expressed previously. There is a two-tier support system. The academic tutor on a course takes on the role of personal tutor for the duration of the course and the programme tutor provides continuity in supporting the student throughout the MSc programme. Course tutors are the first contact about matters that affect a student's studies. This course tutor can prompt silent students to check that they are progressing. Alternatively, students can choose to contact the programme tutor or administrator and typically do so if they are thinking of dropping out. The students are almost entirely mature students and are coping with work pressures. The personal problems presented can be serious, as is characteristic of part time students and have included family problems, redundancy, relocation or moving house and financial difficulties. Other problems are academic and skills-based, particularly if the student cannot express them in a way that allows the tutor to provide immediate help.

Eight staff: seven academic tutors, including the programme tutor, and the programme administrator were interviewed. Staff marked their answers to questions, the majority of which employed a 5-point Likert scale during the interview (eg 1 = strongly disagree to 5 = strongly agree). We give the median score for the questions unless otherwise indicated. There was also a small number of yes/no questions such as 'Would you ask a colleague for advice with student problems if necessary?'. Four main areas were explored in the questionnaire:

- settling students in and promoting a sense of belonging
- dealing with students' personal and study problems
- the advantages and disadvantages of the online environment and email
- staff time-management for personal tutoring.

In addition, the questionnaire provided space for comments and examples and the interviewer asked for further information and for these to be clarified if necessary.

Staff views of personal tutoring online
Establishing relationships

Staff were unsure whether it is more difficult to know if students have settled in online rather than on-campus [median 3], with some staff commenting that both are equally difficult. Comments were made that it is possible to get some indication online by monitoring when students log on to the system but not seeing the students face-to-face is a problem, together with the difficulty of getting class discussions going.

McCartan (2000) reports that online teaching staff can find the feeling of their remoteness from students unrewarding and consequently may retreat to delivering content alone, rather than building relationships with students (Conrad, 2004). However, staff in our study strongly agreed that most students do achieve a sense of belonging during the course [median 4.5] and interact with each other [median 4], though they felt that this interaction was more difficult for tutors to promote online [median 3.5]. They disagreed with the statement that it is more difficult for online students to initiate interaction with staff [median 2], mentioning email and class discussion. Two tutors mentioned the importance of giving out some limited personal information to students. Other strategies for facilitating successful online communication with students will be considered further at the end of this chapter.

Staff strongly disagreed with the statement that communication was impeded by the technology used [median1] whereas in an earlier study staff perceptions on an online Records Management Masters programme were dominated by problems with the technology (McCartan, 2000). This may be due to advances in technology and the confidence with technology of these Masters Computer Science students. It must also be noted that student numbers in the early stages of the programme have so far been fairly small with 32 students at the time the staff interviews took place.

Student problems

Student problems brought to staff were categorised as study or personal problems. Sub-categories of study problems were: lack of self-motivation to study, time-management problems, study skills problems, lack of pre-requisite academic skills, English language problems and 'other'. Personal problems were sub-categorised as health, family, relationship, employment, financial problems and other problems.

Study problems

Overall staff reported being consulted on all sub-categories of study problems, particularly study skills, time management and English language problems, plus problems caused by cultural and academic differences and expectations. Staff reported that students were highly motivated but that there were often problems with balancing the demands of work, family and study. Some students had difficulty in understanding what was needed in an assessment. Cultural and institutional differences in educational practices and procedures were also felt to cause difficulties.

Personal problems

Overall, staff reported being consulted on all sub-categories of personal problem, except the 'other' category, with the programme tutor and administrator being consulted on a wider range than the module tutors: two module tutors had not been consulted about any personal issues. This underlines the importance of including administrators in online personal tutoring training programmes.

Family problems, relationship problems, employment problems and financial problems predominated. Employment problems were also reported as a subject of student online discussion and were the main cause of withdrawal for part time students in HE (Yorke, 2000). One concern raised was that some students might withdraw without approaching tutors. Sosabowski *et al* (2003), in a study of on-campus students, found that a few students did not want to share problems with tutors, which perhaps indicated a need for direct links to central student services.

Dealing with student problems

Staff agreed that it is more difficult to help students with study problems online than face-to-face [median 4] and strongly agreed that it is more difficult for personal problems [median 4.5]. For study problems staff mentioned difficulties in running a student's computer programme online and talking through a solution. Lack of immediacy was also an issue; students can have difficulty in stating their problem and giving all the relevant information. Synchronous communication software might alleviate some problems but this can be difficult to arrange due to time zone differences and it is costly in staff time. For personal problems staff said that although having time to find out how to help a student before responding was advantageous, it was hard to counsel students online and that they were more likely to be forthcoming face-to-face.

Staff support

University resources were believed to provide fairly adequate support for personal tutoring staff [median 2 where 1 = completely adequate], though the difficulty of referring students to the university counselling service and using financial advisors online was mentioned: an online counselling service is due to be piloted on this course. All staff felt able to consult colleagues for help and advice and most had done so: and all academic staff, though not administrative staff, felt able to consult the university counselling service for advice, though none did so.

Communication by email

In our study staff communicated with individual students on personal tutoring issues almost exclusively by email. Generally student telephone contact and personal visits to campus are discouraged, and rarely used, as the course is seen as being exclusively online, though many distance learning courses do use several communication channels, especially for personal tutoring purposes.

Email, as an asynchronous mode of communication has both advantages and disadvantages for personal tutoring. Romiszowski and Mason (2002), in a review of research, note that discourse functions, used in computer-mediated asynchronous communication, appear to be more limited than in synchronous communication, though the grammar used is likely to be richer and more complex with greater time available for thought. There may be gender differences in email use, with females finding it easier to write about feelings and relationships than males. Oravec (2000), discussing psycho-therapy and counselling by email, mentions the need to help clients accus-tomed to computers to shift their communication style from the unedited and terse to the more carefully considered; the lack of tonal cues on email can also lead to the misinterpretation of messages. Barker (2002), from the point of view of online academic tutors, notes that it is easy to be misunderstood on email, particularly when trying to express feelings and ideas. Robson and Robson (2000) discuss the impact on email counselling of the loss of visual and non-verbal cues for communicating feelings and emotions, with emo-ticons being a poor substitute. However, writing problems down can be beneficial to the client in promoting reflection and in distinguishing between the external and the client's self. Email communication also has the advan-tage of being fast and always available. All of these issues are likely to have an effect on online personal tutoring.

Generally, email communication was felt by staff in our study, who were very experienced computer and email users, to be helpful when dealing with per-sonal tutoring issues. Nevertheless, the asynchronous nature of email, with the lack of instant response and feedback, was seen as causing moderate dif-ficulties for effective communication. The programme tutor and adminis-trator, who dealt with the biggest range of student personal problems felt it caused great difficulties. However, an advantage which was pointed out was that there was enough time to think responses through before replying.

Staff generally thought that the written English language skills of students caused few difficulties for effective email communication. Despite this they reported moderate difficulties due to the lack of face-to-face verbal and non-verbal feedback and clues to meaning and the delay in understanding students' exact meaning, which was caused by having to wait for some time for student responses to requests for clarification. Comments made were that tutors could also be doubtful about the success of a communication and that messages could be misunderstood and needed to be worded carefully.

Issues of online security were felt to cause no difficulties in effective email communication. The reasons given were that the university had its own email server and that students were required to use their university email account, though some students would delay looking at their email. However, there were also comments about having to be guarded about what was said, though most tutors felt that the issue of creating a written record of interaction caused no difficulties for effective communication.

Staff attitudes to the online environment for personal tutoring

Generally, the academic staff, module tutors and the programme tutor, found the lack of face-to-face contact with their students unhelpful in dealing with personal tutoring issues [median 2]. In general they were undecided as to whether the online environment had more or less advantages for staff and students than the face-to-face environment [median 3]. They cited the difficulty of asking direct questions and getting immediate responses which tended to lead to them having to believe everything written, because of the difficulty and delay in questioning it, the lack of informal feedback and face-to-face contact, also the difficulty of typing everything they wanted to say because of the time it took and the online accessibility of the tutor. This led to some students asking the tutor for easily available information without looking for it first. On the plus side, staff felt that they could give answers in their own time and could easily include information from lecture notes for students with study problems. It was also acknowledged by some staff that some students might prefer not to have face-to-face contact and that students could express themselves in their own time and manage their time well.

The ability to respond to and initiate online email communication at their own pace was found very helpful by all staff [median 5], with staff mentioning the space it gives to think about and research a problem before responding, though they also mentioned the importance of sending an immediate holding response first. Generally personal tutoring staff were undecided as to whether they felt more or less in control online than in the on-campus environment [median 3] and felt that it took longer to deal with student issues and problems online. Issues raised included the time taken to type as opposed to speak, the need to be careful with what was written down, the delay in clarifying details and getting responses and the greater possibility of misunderstanding. On the other hand an immediate email response could be sent, without the student having to wait for a face-to-face appointment. Other studies have reported that successful online programmes promoting

143

student and staff interaction appear to take much more staff time than face-to-face programmes (eg Fuks *et al*, 2001; Mason and Weller, 2000), so that it is not surprising that online personal tutoring can also be seen as much more time-consuming.

Conclusions

Although numbers are small and results not generalisable, some interesting indications emerge. Whilst these computer science staff recognised advantages in the online environment and were happy to use email to communicate with students over personal tutoring issues, they felt that email imposed certain constraints when it was the only, or main medium of communication. There seemed to be some frustration caused by the sense of distance from the student and of the sense of time and effort needed to be spent because of the potential difficulties of achieving clear and successful communication on what could be sensitive issues. The reduction of available cues as to how the student was feeling and reacting to the communication, or even sometimes not knowing if it was received at all, were an issue with staff having to tolerate more uncertainty than might be the case in face-to-face interaction. Some staff felt that students might also find communication more difficult and that this might lead to more students with problems dropping out, rather than approaching staff for help.

Nevertheless, staff felt that they could build online relationships with students and had developed strategies to promote staff/student communication, such as limited personal disclosure – for instance as 'I live in X town', or 'I'm just popping out to lunch now' – the use of a more informal oral language style; the use of emoticons to help convey feelings; speedy replies. They liked being able to deal with student communications at their own pace and in their own time, to give them time to research any complex issues involved.

Recommendations

What needs to be considered is whether online personal tutoring, where feasible, is better supplemented by phone or by face-to-face communication as is often usual with distance-learning courses, or other technological methods, such as webcams and Voice over IP (VoIP), as they become reliable. It would also seem advisable, with the increasing development of online courses, to offer specialist online personal tutor training as a matter of course to both academic and administrative staff, as it is likely that the programme administrator will be consulted by students on personal tutoring issues as they are there. Such courses might consider ways of helping staff cope with the uncertainty inherent in online personal tutoring by training staff in useful strategies to help build relationships with students when communicating with them online, especially asynchronously, and to compensate for the lack of verbal and non-verbal feedback. Rekkedal (1997) reports on a Norwegian training course for online tutors, which is itself online and so builds on tutors' experience of being online students themselves so they can better understand their students' experience.

Liu and Ginther (2002) maintain the importance of impression management in computer-mediated communication (CMC) and discuss linguistic and communicative strategies for overcoming the lack of face-to-face channels of feedback. They discuss research, indicating that CMC has features of both verbal and written language, which result in verbal and non-verbal cues which, interacting with the context of the message, contribute to developing interpersonal relationships. They recommend course tutors to use various verbal and non-verbal communicative strategies, which we have interpreted as follows:

Verbal strategies
- follow CMC language norms for greetings and expression of attitudes and ideas
- use appropriate language style for the type of message. For interpersonal messages use an interpersonal rather than a formal style
- consider the needs of the student and adapt the message content accordingly
- express attitudes appropriately by relating to the topic of the message and avoiding too neutral a tone where possible. Avoid too much hedging, hesitation, use of tag-questions and over-politeness
- avoid insults and strong direct criticism
- when replying to a message, control emotions aroused if feeling attacked or insulted

Nonverbal Strategies
- reply reasonably rapidly to messages and avoid being too terse
- open and close messages in a friendly positive way, using nicknames if appropriate
- use emoticons, pictographs and typographic marks where appropriate to express attitudes and feelings about the topic of the message
- check typing and spelling errors to avoid misunderstanding and of giving an impression of carelessness and incompetence

These strategies indicate a way in which some of the disadvantages of online, as compared to face-to-face communication can be compensated for, though this is an evolving field of research.

Staff also need to feel supported by the institution in their personal tutoring role, not only by the provision of online personal tutoring training but also by provision of online and student-friendly access to institutional student support services (Wiesenberg, 2001). In view of the evidence that access to support services can help prevent attrition and enhance the student experience (Promnitz and Germain, 1996), institutions need also to support staff by making adequate resources available including recognition of the extra time involved in online personal tutoring.

14

Working with a lack of structure: The experience of supporting work based learning

Charlotte Ramage

Introduction

Staffing shortages within the health care sector which affect release from the workplace, increasing distances between clinical settings and the university and a rapidly changing health culture, have challenged traditional ways of designing and delivering educational courses within higher education. More specifically, the growth of National Occupational Standards and the emergence of Skills for Health have substantively changed the way higher education now views education within the health care professions. New, more responsive, flexible modes of meeting individuals' learning needs have been called for in the form of work-based and online learning (DoH, 2001, 2002). Within this context the role of lecturer as conveyor of expert knowledge becomes sidelined in favour of a role that has received little attention in the literature: that of the personal tutor. It is the skills inherent in the personal tutor role: as facilitator, guide, assessor and supporter, that respond to the needs of learners who are engaged in these relatively new modes of learning.

The role of the educationalist in supporting work-based learning is neglected in the literature, yet it is uniquely placed in the higher education institution to bridge academic and professional worlds and reflect the partnership working between learners, the workplace and higher education.

In our organisation, we have established a work-based learning framework, supporting a range of modules that will respond to the scope of work-based activity, reflecting technical activity – developing skills and interpretative activity – encouraging learning through reflective practice and strategic activity and involving the critical evaluation of values and beliefs which encourage collaborative working and exchange of ideas and which lead to changes in organisational working (Gray *et al*, 2004). The work-based learning framework has now been active for three years with ever increasing numbers of learners enrolling on the modules. A robust method of evaluation was considered important at this stage, to clarify whether the modules really did meet the expectations of all those involved.

This chapter reports on the findings of an ongoing qualitative research study, using grounded theory to explore the roles of teachers, mentors and learners who engaged in work-based learning activity. The aim of the research is to generate understanding about the nature of these roles and the factors that hinder and facilitate their development. Grounded theory is an appropriate methodological approach for exploring roles and role relationships. By processing the concerns of subjects and moving beyond description to conceptualisation, grounded theory can account for and interpret the main patterns of action and provide explanations for the major variations in behaviour in the area of study (Glaser, 1992; Charmaz, 1994). The explanations that emerge can provide a level of understanding and control which may pave the way for action and change. It is hoped that the findings will assist both higher education and hospital and primary care trusts in developing and supporting the roles of those involved in work-based learning.

Descriptive data were collected through in-depth face-to-face interviews. These interviews were recorded and the data transcribed verbatim and analysed, using the grounded theory analytical techniques of constant comparison. The research findings to date have arisen from interviews with five educational advisors, three learners and one mentor.

The data gathered from teachers has shown that their role is about a need for structure, being a facilitator of learning, learning to learn and that the core category is realising the learning. One example, which illustrates how the categories interrelate, is that learners appeared to want clear guidance to indicate how they should progress with their learning. The learners' need for clear guidance could impact on the role of teacher as facilitator, as the teachers found that they were giving information and telling the learner how to manage their learning, as opposed to facilitating the learner to develop their own learning. The learners' behaviour arose from initial concerns about this new mode of learning. It wasn't until they realised how to manage their own learning that the teacher could truly facilitate the learning process. Once all those involved had completed the learning programme, they were able to see the value of the experience and recognise the learning that had been archived. At this point they became confident about the process.

This chapter will focus on the category 'A need for structure' because it more clearly identifies the developmental needs of the teacher who is engaged in supporting learners who are enrolled on work-based learning modules.

The term learner is deliberately used to denote the change in relationship from student to learner. In work-based learning, the learner is constructing and managing their own learning experience in the workplace. It was felt that this shift in role responsibility should be recognised. So should the fact that the term educational advisor is used instead of teacher or personal tutor, as it was felt that this term more aptly recognises the skills involved in the role. There is a similar discussion in the work of Phillips (1994), who considers that the role of the personal tutor should be renamed facilitator of learning, as the title captures the activity involved in the role more appropriately.

A need for structure

The research has revealed that a need for structure is a phenomenon experienced by all educational advisors, learners and mentors when they first engage with work-based learning. The experience arose from a perceived need for clear guidelines to help those involved to manage the open nature of learning through work that appeared to lack the structure of conventional forms of learning, with pre-set learning outcomes and defined content. All of those who were involved in work-based learning seemed to cope better when some kind of framework was developed, through which the learning could be structurally developed, monitored and kept on track. The educational advisor's role in this process was to offer support and guidance.

Educational advisors provided guidance and support in various ways: they offered help with the development of the learning contract, which encouraged active engagement with the learning process. The learners were also provided with online learning units in the managed learning environment (MLE). These directed them to test out the use of reflective strategies to promote learning through work and to encourage them to explore their environment, practice and relationships within the workplace. Action learning sets and tutorials were also offered to encourage intra-professional sharing, support and reassurance. Vygotsky (1978) refers to this as scaffolding. Scaffolding the student experience is essential if learners are to reach out and extend their existing technical skill and understanding of their role within the field of practice.

Educational advisors saw the qualities of guiding and supporting the learner through the process of learning as most closely resembling the activity of the personal tutor.

> I think that the skills required for the educational advisor, a lot of them ... seem to fit in with the role of the personal tutor, in that you are offering guidance and support, getting the person to think through for themselves what the best action would be, but then I think that is what a good personal tutor is, you are not here with the answers, you are there to reflect back to the student 'What do you think you should do about this?' (educational advisor)

The role of advisor as a guide for learners and mentors was crucial in building confidence in the self-managed approach to learning through work. At the outset it was important for the educational advisor to clarify the framework through which the learning experience could be managed through tripartite meetings with the mentor and learner. Setting up the conditions for partnership working was essential to clarify new roles, role relationships and responsibilities in engaging with work-based learning. Both mentor and learner needed to understand and feel confident about identifying, managing and assessing learning opportunities in practice. The role relationships and responsibilities could then be clarified through the learning contract.

This chapter addresses these issues by exploring the use of learning contracts, strategies for keeping the learner on track and issues about maintaining learning in the workplace through guided learning in practice.

The learning contract

Educational advisors, mentors and learners clearly considered that early development of the learning contract was pivotal regarding the ability of the learner to progress forward with their learning. Within this section the value of the learning contract is explored in providing a structure for the learning experience.

The learning contract is important because it engenders dialogue and partnership-working through the concept of negotiated learning which is considered to be the most important element of the process, irrespective of the format chosen to record the learning. Contract learning also enabled the learner to structure their learning experience.

> Until you have your outcomes in your head you don't know when you will want your study days and what you want to do with them. (learner)

By involving the learner in the process of workplace curriculum design from the outset, contract learning encourages the concept of an active learner. Biggs (1989), Knowles (1975) and Donaldson (1992) considered that the learner who was actively engaged in designing their own learning learned more and better than those who preferred to wait passively to be taught.

> It makes you read more and learn more than you would on a taught module. (learner)

The educational advisor's role in the development of the learning contract is to guide learners and mentors through the process of contract development, the identification of learning outcomes and the processes by which these learning outcomes can be met through resources, activities and assessment of evidence. To encourage active engagement with learning, the educational advisor clarifies the conditions for ownership of the learning process and solicits mutual agreement on areas of personal responsibility (Richardson, 1987). This form of negotiated learning reflects a truly individualised bespoke package of learning, as it is designed so it takes account of the context of the workplace, the workplace environment and the specific needs of the learner. The educational advisor then ensures that the terminology and scope of the learning outcomes are consistent with academic levels and the amount of credit claimed.

Educational advisors could at times feel anxious about the significance of their role in developing confidence in mentors and learners to support contract learning. They worried about whether they had got it right.

> I think it is just that we are not quite used to the idea of making learning outcomes ....or what could be included as learning outcomes and what could be included as skills or competencies. (educational advisor)

This problem for teachers may have its origins in the very nature of learner directed learning. Contract learning promotes learning by discovery. Through this process teachers are no longer expected to control the learning (Gibbon, 1989). This may have led to a sense of vulnerability about what their role was. The confusion about skills and competencies possibly reflects the difficulty teachers have in judging what valued knowledge is. Educational advisors, as well as learners, need to learn to re-orientate their traditional teaching role, from information dissemination to facilitation and advising (Richardson, 1987).

Donaldson (1992) identified that students could also feel anxious about contract learning and in order to maintain interest and commitment to the contract they needed help in making that transition from teacher-centred to student-centred learning.

> To start with it is very confusing with what you are doing, because it is an empty box and perhaps you don't know what it is you want to learn. (learner)

> They were really scared by it and said 'We just want you to tell us what to do'. (educational advisor)

The educational advisor therefore needs to facilitate the learner through the process of becoming more self-directed and through supporting the learner, to enable them to feel confident that their own learning is valid. Rogers (1983) considered that significant learning was only possible when individuals had the self-confidence in their own ability to learn and felt that the learning experience would be rewarding and meaningful.

Keeping the learner on track

The concept of keeping the learning on track reflects the educational advisor's strategy for supporting and monitoring the progress of the learner and making sure that they have access to resources that promote their learning.

All the educational advisors in the study chose to use action learning to manage the learning process. The use of action learning supported the facilitative role of the educational advisor in encouraging networking, risk taking, testing out of ideas about practice and peer sharing in a supportive environment (McGill and Beatty, 1995).

> She [a learner] gave information on the issue of consent for procedures and she worked in a theatre environment and we were talking about consent for minor procedures and she gave the information to the learner in the urology investigations unit. So there is a very rich sharing of expertise there. (educational advisor)

It was clear that the action learning sets also provided a means through which the educational advisor could monitor progress and keep the learner on track with their learning.

> ..the other thing I do at the end of each session is [to] ask them to set their agenda item for the next time so they have something to go away with. ...I

> also get them to document what they achieved from their action learning set and what they plan to do. That does tend to make them quite self-directed in what they intend to do in the intervening period. (educational advisor)

Action learning sets mirror the personal tutor role in supervising the learning through tutorials. If an educational advisor could not organise the groups, due to the small numbers of learners, they offer personal tutorial time. This, like the action learning sets, provides the learner with a structured support system through which they can manage their learning

> I don't know how I could have done it without the tutorial support, because, that as well as the mentorship was pulling everything together and making sure I was going in the right direction. (learner)

The initial concern for educational advisors facilitating action learning was whether they had the relevant knowledge to respond to questions about areas of practice with which they were unfamiliar.

> The first time I put my action learning set together I was a bit uncomfortable with it because I still have this idea that I need to be an expert in their areas of practice ... I did have to take a step back and think, is this more about how I enable people and I really did start to understand the meaning of facilitation. (educational advisor)

This feeling of discomfort arises from two key areas: a challenge to self as expert and self as capable of facilitating learning. Teachers in higher education institutions are organised into the subjects they teach, which form a major part of their identity (Eraut, 2004). The learners in an action learning set challenge this identity of expert because they come from varying intradisciplinary backgrounds with differing learning needs. Secondly, the conflict with self as expert versus self as facilitator is mirrored by Knowles (1975, p33) who acknowledged that he found this transition from teacher to facilitator of learning terribly difficult and had 'to resist the need to pose as the expert who had mastered any given body of content' and instead join the student honestly as a co-learner.

Another approach intended to keep learning on track was the use of online learning units through the managed learning environment (MLE). Online learning mirrors the facilitative role of the educational advisor in that the teacher experiences a shift in the sharing of knowledge from teacher to learner, to the teacher enabling the learner to construct knowledge themselves. This is supported in a study by Christianson et al (2002) where the teachers described their role in online learning as a coach or mentor, rather than being the person who simply conveys the information. The key issue in developing learning materials online is to design tasks that will help the learner to structure their activities and encourage thinking about discussing and applying concepts in the workplace and in evidencing their learning. However, the educational advisor needs to guard against over-enthusiasm and be mindful of the volume of learning activity generated through activities because online learning should enhance and facilitate the learning experience, rather than overload curriculum content which is predominantly situated in the workplace (Ramage, 2005).

Guided learning in practice

The concept of guided learning in practice addresses some of the problematic issues associated with the situated learning environment (Lave and Wenger, 1991). The educational advisor found that it could be difficult to control how learning was managed in practice: this meant that advisors had to get more involved with the workplace to encourage learning communities, with professionals sharing their expertise and willingness to work with the learners, and to develop learning opportunities through work.

Supporting learners to identify meaningful learning when they are new to their field of practice could take time. The length of time taken to develop the learning contract surprised teachers and is noted by Jarvis (1995) as one of the key problems in managing contract learning for large groups of students. The learners needed a clear mind to clarify what they needed to learn and this was the only possible way to do it, by experiencing their professional role in practice. Until they had engaged with the nature of practice, it was impossible for them to articulate their learning needs or to reflect on their learning.

> ...you can't write about things until they have happened, and until you have learnt skills you can't really reflect on them. It's an ever increasing thing. (learner)

Billett (1996) found that only through exposure to participation in vocational tasks, could the learner with the guidance of expert others, work out tentative solutions, which would lead to a more detailed understanding of the procedures required to be successful in those tasks. This argument is about *poesis versus praxis* (Carr, 1987): instead of imposing theory on practice, the learner looked for the kind of social engagements to provide the proper context for learning. The generation of work-related knowledge does not reflect the standard paradigm of knowledge that values abstract thought, a universal understanding of knowledge and transparency (Hager, 2004). It relies on the application of context-specific knowledge, skills needed for competence (Eraut, 2004), understanding of other people and their situation and organisational environment, their decision-making and practical judgement (Eraut, 2004 and Hager, 2004). Workplace knowledge involves collaborative dialogue through social engagement in communities of practice (Lave and Wenger, 1991; Gheradi *et al*, 1998; Hager, 2004). It is clear that the learner requires practical knowledge of their work before they can articulate what they need to learn in learning outcome statements. It also shows that the mentor role is crucial in creating opportunities for learning through work, by providing access to practice and increasingly complex tasks, through coaching, modelling and scaffolding-learning experiences (Collins *et al*, 1989 and Vygotsky, 1978).

Structuring the learning experience in the workplace was problematic though it was due to a variety of factors such as variable support from a mentor, poor collegiate support for the mentorship role and lack of resources to support learning in the workplace. Cahill (1996) noted these concerns and felt that the considerable variation in availability of the mentor and their interest in the learner resulted in superficial relationships and was a reflection of the lack of support which nurses received for their mentorship role.

There was no doubt that poor or indifferent mentor support impacted negatively on the ability of the learner to progress forward with their learning programme (Miller and Blackman, 2004).

Learners affirmed that the role of mentor was not valued in practice:

> The trouble is your colleagues do not seem to want to recognise the need for mentor time. (learner)

Learners considered that the need for the mentor to recognise that they needed time to reflect away from practice was important:

> I can see how you might be able to work with someone in action, sort of work with them and dialogue with them in the moment but if you need to reflect in more detail about issues in practice you need to come away. You can't do that in-depth reflection as you are doing it. (learner)

However, coming away was problematic because practice areas did not always accept the need for two people to leave.

> I think when it is one person coming up to talk to you for example an educational advisor, then that is looked on differently. But when it is two people from the same area, the tendency is to think it isn't important. (learner)

It seemed that mentors experienced constant interruptions when they did try to get away to reflect more deeply on practice with a learner.

155

> It's no use using the seminar room because they come and find you ... some-one knocks on the door 'the GP is on the phone can you take this call?' (mentor)

Little has changed since Jarvis (1992) highlighted the problem that health care settings provided neither the systems nor the time required by nurses to promote reflection on their practice.

When mentorship was indifferent, it took learners longer to learn, a view supported by Miller and Blackman (2004). This situation led to a start/stop mode of learning that was initially bewildering and frustrating for the educational advisor's who saw this as the key difference between their role as personal tutors and work-based advisors, that however much support the educational advisor gave, it was the conditions in the workplace that predominantly influenced the learner's ability to progress. This finding is also mirrored in the work of Miller and Blackman (2004), who found that when mentors did not provide learners with feedback on their progress and showed little interest in the learner's needs, the learner was plunged into self-doubt and lacked direction.

Another important issue relating to learning through work was that access to computers to support online learning in the workplace was so limited. Access was needed so that learners could interact with the learning materials and access the online library.

> There is a problem with access. There are very few PC's available, maybe only one or two in the ward area and it's hard to access them for learning support. (senior manager)

The withdrawal of learners from work-based learning modules indicated that poor mentorship support could influence a learner's decision to drop out from the module. However, when mentorship was good, the learner's confidence and self-esteem rose significantly:

> My experience of mentorship has been very positive... In situations that are new to me she doesn't come in and take over... she pushes me forward and says you can do it. I will be here if you want advice... It was great to know she was in the background supporting me and having faith in me to do the right thing. She isn't bothered if I don't know, she just says let's talk about what we have learnt from this situation. (learner)

In order to maintain the learning in the practice area, the educational advisor would work closely with the mentors to clarify the learning agreement and provide additional information on their role expectations. They found this aspect of their role quite resource intensive.

> Talking to some of the mentors, you need to put a lot more time aside for just discussion using you as a sounding board. (educational advisor)

However, they were also able to see that this kind of facilitative support reaped rewards.

> She was a really good mentor in the end [she had initially been anxious and needed a lot of support] and actually she is now mentoring one of the work based learning project nurses because she has supported students before... I think she is really good. She has some good ideas and seems to understand what is expected of the student. (educational advisor)

Philips (1994) recognised the equal importance of the combination of the support mechanism provided by the mentor and the personal tutor in maximising the student's learning potential. This was no less significant for the educational advisor, mentor and learner tripartite relationship in work-based learning. The study revealed that educational advisors viewed maintaining the learning experience in the workplace as problematic. Yet once learners became more self-directed through contract learning, they learned to be more assertive about their learning needs and developed strategies to overcome indifferent attitudes to their learning (Gibbon, 1989).

> It pushed me to learn skills and develop knowledge in those skills and actually push areas, where for example where I was doing venepuncture and I couldn't get in to do any practice but it wasn't until I pushed the right people and said 'Look I need to do this. I have got to get in to do this' that I was allowed, you know. That made me more determined... (learner)

The situatedness of the curriculum in the workplace remains an area of concern for educational advisors (Lave and Wenger, 1991; Gherardi *et al*, 1998). If the government wants to shift professional development away from higher education to the workplace, through vocational and competency-based skill learning, championed by Skills for Health, and through e-learning and work based learning (DoH, 2001), the role of the mentor needs recognition within the new nursing grade bands, to increase its sense of value within the workplace. There also needs to be provision of learning areas and access to computer resources for learning support. All these have been highlighted in previous government documents but it is clear that access to these resources remains problematic (DoH, 2001; DoH, 2002).

Conclusion

The factors that influence the need for structure within this grounded theory study, exploring the role of the educational advisor in work-based learning, have been discussed in this chapter. One of the key areas of interest is the extent of support needed to facilitate learners and mentors in developing learning contracts and that all those involved need sustained support in the early stages of contract design. In our organisation we encourage educational advisors and mentors to share their experiences of developing learning contracts through workshop activity and have set deadlines for learning contracts to be handed in for formative feedback. We have also stated that the learners need to revisit the learning contract half way through their module, so that initially they can focus on two learning outcomes until they have a clearer idea about more specific learning they want to engage in. This sets a deadline for the learners to work to and also allows them to experience the world of practice and discover further learning needs through a more prolonged engagement with work.

This highlights another concern related to the situatedness of learning: that learners may only have peripheral access to learning opportunities, due to poor support from mentors and professional colleagues. To accommodate this dynamic, we have extended the time line for module completion to eleven months, to allow for the effect of dynamics in the workplace influencing the learners' progression with their learning programme.

Another factor highlighted in the research study was the use of online learning resources. Developing good online learning units and resources, to help signpost learning activities for the learner in the workplace, is an ongoing activity in the work-based learning team. We have found that teachers need the confidence to gain new skills in translating traditional ways of managing teaching sessions into activities that will help the learners to explore their professional roles in practice. In response to this need our organisation promotes engagement with online learning through workshop opportunities on the use of Blackboard, our virtual learning environment and the use of programmes designed to help to create online learning resources such as Course Genie which is a programme that helps to convert word documents into professional looking e-learning units.

Teachers are also helped to imagine innovative ways of developing e-learning materials through a university programme which encourages lecturers to share their work through workshop activity and offering guests access to their module resources online.

Finally, mentors and educational advisors are all encouraged to attend a work-based project group, set up to support mentors, educational advisors and modules leaders who are engaged in work-based learning activities. The group facilitates good networking relationships, partnership-working between practice and the higher education institution, and also fosters good practice through research and evaluation of work-based learning experiences.

I intend to continue data collection to explore the role of the learner and mentor in work-based learning. By shedding light on these roles we may better understand how to support learners and mentors and how to develop an understanding of how learners are learning in the workplace and what the conditions are that support learning. This research is timely due to the current emphasis on competence-based education in the workplace as a measure of fitness for purpose.

Postscript
Liz Thomas

This book has brought together research, investigation and evaluation about personal tutoring and advising to support students in higher education in the UK in the 21st century. It demonstrates that while there is a dearth of published material about tutoring, there is a great deal of innovation and development taking place in the sector and this is accompanied by a significant amount of institutional research. This is research which explores the issues: it pilots new interventions and evaluates the impact of change within the institutional setting. This work not only offers important data for institutional development but, at the aggregate level, is a valuable resource that can benefit the sector as a whole. There is however a need for further research on many of the issues discussed here.

The chapters in this book provide a strong evidence base to inform the development of personal tutoring policy and practice, both within higher education institutions and nationally. Personal tutoring has an important role to play to enhance students' learning experience in HE and to improve retention, progression and success. Traditional models of tutoring are no longer appropriate or fit for the purpose. Therefore this requires institutions to adopt new models of personal tutoring which are student-centred, integrated in learning, connected to professional services and proactively engaging students, especially as they make the transition into HE. Staff need to be involved in the development of new tutoring systems and provided with guidance, training and support to enable them to fulfil their new roles, in a wider range of contexts and modes of delivery than ever before.

References

Archer, L., Hutchings, M., Ross, A., Leathwood, C., Gilchrist, R. and Phillips, D. (2003) *Higher Education and Social Class: issues of exclusion and inclusion*. London: Routledge Falmer

Aynsley-Smith, S. (2002) Widening participation and student support. *Learning and Teaching in Action* (Manchester Metropolitan University), 1 (1) pp3-8

Ball, S. J. and Rowe, R. (1991) Micropolitics of Radical Change, in Blase, J. (ed) *The Politics of Life in Schools: Power, Conflict and Cooperation*. London: Sage

Bamber, J. and Tett, L. (2000) 'Transforming the learning experiences of non-traditional students: A perspective from higher education', *Studies in Continuing Education*, 22(1): 57-75.

Barker, M. (2000) Student Loneliness: Findings of a Longitudinal Study. Presentation to The Student Well-Being Conference, University of Glasgow, August 31st and September 1st, 2000

Barker, P. (2002) On Being an Online Tutor. *Innovations in Education and Teaching International*. Routledge. 39 (1), pp.3-13

Barlow, J. and Antoniou, M. (2003) *The experience of new lecturers at the University of Brighton*, Centre for Learning and Teaching, University of Brighton

Barlow, J. and Antoniou, M. (forthcoming) Room for improvement: the experiences of new lecturers in higher education. *Innovations in Education and Teaching International*

Biggs, J. (1989) Approaches to enhancement of tertiary teaching. *Higher Education Research and Development*. 8 7-27

Billet, S. (1996) Towards a model of workplace learning: the learning curriculum. *Studies in Continuing Education*. 18(1) 43-58

Blasko, Z, Brennan, J, Little, B. and Shah, T. (2003), *Access to what: analysis of factors determining graduate employability*. London: Centre for Higher Education research

Blythman, M, and Orr, S. (2002) A Framework for Institutional Change, in Hayton, A. and Paczuska, A. (eds) *Access, Participation and Higher Education*. London: Kogan Page

Bournemouth University (2005) Hurne, J. personal communication

Bourdieu, P. (1997) The Forms of Capital, in Halsey, A.H, Lauder, H. Brown, P. and Wells, A.S. (eds) *Education: Culture, Economy and Society*. Oxford: Oxford University Press

Butler, R. (1988) Enhancing and undermining intrinsic motivation; the effects of task-involving and ego-involving evaluation on interest and performance. *British journal of educational psychology* 58 pp 1-14

Cahill, H. (1996) A qualitative analysis of student nurses' experiences of mentorship. *Journal of Advanced Nursing*. 24. 791-799

Cantor, L., Roberts, L., Pratley, B. (1995) *A Guide to Further Education in England and Wales.* London: Cassell

Carr, W. (1987) What is an educational practice? *Journal of Philosophy of Education.* 21(2): 167-175

Case, P. and Elliot, B. (1997) Attrition and Retention in distance learning programs, problems strategies, problems and solutions. *Open Praxis* 1 pp30-33.

Challenger-Gillett, J. (2005) Personal tutoring and student retention: the small group tutorial strategy adopted in Computing at the University of Brighton Higher Education Academy Personal Tutoring Conference, London, May 2005

Chapman, D. (2003) keynote presentation at the National Student Retention Conference, San Diego, California www.noel-levitz.com accessed 4 November 2005.

Charmaz, K. (1994) The grounded theory method: an explication and interpretation, in Glaser, B. (ed) *More Grounded theory methodology: a reader.* California: Sociological Press

Christianson, L. Tiene, D and Luft, P. (2002) Web based teaching in undergraduate nursing programs. *Nurse Education Today.* 27(6) 276-282

Claxton, G. (1999) *Wise Up: The Challenge of Lifelong Learning,* New York: Bloomsbury

Collins, A, Brown, J. and Newman, S. (1989) Cognitive apprenticeship: teaching the crafts of reading, writing and mathematics, in Resnick, l. (ed) *Knowing, learning and instruction, essays in honour of Robert Glaser.* Hillsdale, New Jersey: Erlbaum and Associates.

Collins, R. and Lim, H. (2003a) *The Challenge of Transition.* LTSN Briefing Paper available at http://www.heacademy.ac.uk/resources.asp?process=full_recordandsection=generic andid=306, accessed 18th January 2005

Collins, R. and Lim, H. (2003b) Student Support Network and Spiral Induction Evaluation, Unpublished report, Southampton Institute

Conrad, D. (2004) University Instructors' Reflections on their First Online Teaching Experiences. *Journal of Asynchronous Learning Networks* Vol.8, Issue 2 pp.31-44. http://www.sloan-c.org/publications/jaln/index.asp accessed April 2005

Cooke, R., Barkham, M., Audin, K., Bradley, M. and Davy, J. (2004) 'How social class differences affect students' experience of university', *Journal of Further and Higher Education,* 28(4): 407-421.

Covington, M. V. (1992) *Making the Grade: a Self-Worth Perspective on Motivation and School Reform* Cambridge: Cambridge University Press.

Cowen, R. (1996) Performativity, Post-Modernity and the University. *Comparative Education,* 32 (2), pp.245-258

Crouch, R., Jefferies, A. and Fitzharris, A.M. (1998) Involving the Personal Tutor in Supporting Student Learning. in Rust. C. (ed): *Improving Student Learning – Improving Students as Learners.* Headington, Oxford. Oxford Centre for Staff Development

Crowther, R. and Wootton, S. (2002) *Frameworks for Mentoring – a good practice guide to student mentoring in further and higher education.* The University of Huddersfield

Davies, P. (1999) *Student retention in further education: a problem of quality or of student finance?* Further Education Development Agency. http://www.leeds.ac.uk/educol/documents/00001257.doc

Davies, R. and Elias, P. (2003) *Dropping Out: A Study of Early Leavers from Higher Education.* London: Department of Education and Skills

Dearing report: Report of the National Committee of Inquiry into Higher Education chaired by Sir Ron Dearing, HMSO, 1997; full text also at http://www.leeds.ac.uk/educol/niche/, accessed 1st August 2003

Department for Education and Skills (2003) *The Future of Higher Education* (HM Government White Paper). London: Stationery Office

Department for Education and Skills (2005) *Higher Standards, Better Schools for all* (HM Government White paper). London, Stationery Office

Department of Health (DoH) (2001) *Working together – learning together.* London: DOH

Department of Health (DoH) (2002) *Learning for everyone: A developmental plan for the NHSU: issues for consultation.* London: DoH

Dodgson, R. and Bolam, H. (2002) *Student retention, support and widening participation in the North East of England.* Regional Widening Participation Project, Sunderland, Universities for the North East. www.unis4ne.ac.uk/unew/ProjectsAdditionalFiles/wp/Retention_report.pdf, accessed 15/06/05

Donaldson, I. (1992) The use of learning contracts in the clinical area. *Nurse Education Today.* 12, pp413-436

Dore, R. (1997) *The Diploma Disease.* London: Institute of Education

Earwaker, J. (1992) *Helping and supporting students.* Buckingham, Society for Research into Higher Education and Open University Press

Eaton, S. and Bean, J. (1995) An approach/avoidance behavioural model of college student attrition. *Research in Higher Education,* 36 (6), pp.617-645

Ellsworth, E. (1997) *Teaching Positions.* New York: Teachers College Press

Entwistle, N. J. and Ramsden, P. (1983) *Understanding Student Learning.* London: Croom Helm

Eraut, M. (2004) The transfer of knowledge between education and workplace setting in Rainbird, H, Fuller, A. and Munro, A. (eds). *Workplace learning in context.* London: Routledge

Forsyth, A. and Furlong, A. (2003) *Socio-economic disadvantage and access to higher education.* Bristol: Policy Press

Fuks, H., Gerosa, M.A. and Lucena, C.J.P. (2001) *Sobre o Desenvolvimento e Aplicacao de Cursos Totalmente a Distancia na Internet. Revista Brasileira de Informatica na Educacao.* No. 9. September. Sociedade Brasileira de Computacao pp.61-75 http://www.tandf.co.uk/journals accessed April, 2005

Garvey, B. and Williamson, B. (2002) *Beyond Knowledge Management, Dialogue, creativity and the corporate curriculum.* Harlow: Pearson Education

Gherardi, S, Nicolini D. and Odella, F. (1998) Toward a social understanding of how people learn in organisations: the notion of situated curriculum. *Management Learning.* 29(3): 273-297

Gibbon, C. (1989) Contract learning in a clinical context: report of a case study. *Nurse Education Today.* 9, pp 264-270

Glaser, B. (1992) *Emergence versus forcing. Basics of grounded theory analysis.* California: Sociological Press

Grant, A. (2002) Identifying students' concerns. Taking a whole institutional approach. In N. Stanley and J. Manthorpe (eds) *Students' Mental Health Needs. Problems and Responses.* London: Jessica King Publishers, 83-105.

Grant, A. (2005) The organisation, scale and scope of student service provision in Amosshe member institutions. *Journal of Student Services in Higher Education* (Amosshe), 1, pp.12-20

Grant, A. (in press a) Student services in the United Kingdom – an overview. In Osfield, K. J. and associates (eds) *The Internationalization of Student Affairs and Services in Higher Education: an Emerging Global Perspective*. Washington: NASPA

Grant, A. (in press b): *Mental Health Policies and Practices in UK Higher Education*. London: Universities UK/ Standing Conference of Principals

Grant, A. and Woolfson, M. (2001) Responding to students in difficulty: a cross-institutional collaboration. *Association of University and College Counselling Newsletter and Journal*, 1, 9-11

Gray, D. Cundell, S. and O'Neill J. (2004) *Learning through the workplace: a guide to work-based learning*. Cheltenham: Nelson Thornes

Green, M. (2001) *Successful tutoring: Good practice for managers and tutors*. London: Learning and Skills Development Agency

Grimm, N. (1999) *Good Intentions*. Portsmouth NH: Boynton/Cook

Hager, P. (2004) The conceptualisation and measurement of learning at work, in Rainbird, H. Fuller, A. and Munro, A. (eds). *Workplace learning in context*. London: Routledge

Haggis, T. (2002) Exploring the 'Black Box' of Process: a comparison of theoretical motions of the 'adult learner' with accounts of postgraduate learning experience. *Studies in Higher Education*, 27, pp.207-220

Haggis, T. (2005) Researching difference and particularity: new perspectives from complexity theory, Conference on Challenging the orthodoxies: alternative approaches to educational research. London: December 2005

Hartwell, H. and Farbrother, C. (2004) Enhancing the Learning Environment for Hospitality Students, The Learning and Teaching Conference, ILTHE

Hartwell, H. and Farbrother, C. (2005) Personal Tutor Conference, The Higher Education Academy, http://www.heacademy.ac.uk/3187.htm, accessed January 2006

Harvey, D. (1990) *The Condition of Postmodernity*. Oxford: Blackwell.

HEFCE (2003) *Future needs and support for quality enhancement of learning and teaching in Higher Education*, http://www.hefce.ac.uk/learning/TQEC/final.htm, accessed December 2005

Higgins, R, Hartley, P, and Skelton, A. (2002) The Conscientious Consumer: reconsidering the role of assessment feedback in student learning. *Studies in Higher Education*, 27 (1), pp.53-64

Hill, E. P. (2004) Marks Driving Out Learning: Undergraduate Students' Reactions to the Marks Awarded to Them, Unpublished EdD dissertation, University of Bristol

Hixenbaugh, P., Dewart, H., Drees, D. and Williams, D. (2005) Peer e-mentoring: Enhancement of the first year experience. *Psychology Learning and Teaching*. 5 (1), pp.8-14

House of Commons, Select Committee on Education and Employment, 6th Report, (2001), http://www.parliament.the-stationary-office.co.uk/pa/cm200001/cmselect/cme duemp/124/12402.htm, accessed 10th September 2001

Hoyle, E. (1982) Micropolitics of Educational Organisations. *Educational Management and Administration*, 10, pp.87-98

Jarvis, P. (1992) Reflective practice and nursing. *Nurse Education Today*. 12, pp174-181

Jarvis, P. (1995) *Adult and continuing education: theory and practice*. 2nd edition. London: Routledge and Falmer

Jary, D. (ed) (2002) *Benchmarking and Quality Management: The Debate in UK Higher Education*. Birmingham: C-SAP, Monograph No 1

Joad, C. E. M. (1945) *About Education,* London: Faber and Faber

Juwah, C, Macfarlane-Dick, D, Matthew, B, Nicol, D, Ross, D. and Smith, B. (2004) *Enhancing Student Learning through Effective Formative Feedback*. York: Higher Education Academy http://www.heacademy.ac.uk/senlef.htm, accessed 25/07/05

Knight, P. T. and Yorke, M. (2004) *Learning, Curriculum and Employability in Higher Education*. London: Routledge

Knowles, M. (1975) *Self-directed learning: a guide for learners and teachers*. New York: Association Press

Lago, C. and Shipton, G. (1994) *Personal Tutoring in Action: a handbook for staff who work with and support students*. Sheffield: Sheffield University Counselling Service

Lago, C. and Shipton, G. (1999) *Personal Tutoring in Action* (2nd ed). Sheffield: University of Sheffield

Laing, C. and Robinson, A. (2003) The Withdrawal of Non-traditional Students: developing an explanatory model, *Journal of Further and Higher Education*, 27.2

Lave, J. and Wenger, E. (1991) *Situated learning: Legitimate peripheral participation*. Cambridge: Cambridge University Press.

Layer, G., Srivastava, A., Thomas, L. and Yorke, M. (2002) Student success: Building for change, in Action on Access (eds) *Student Success in Higher Education*. Bradford: University of Bradford

Lea, M. and Street, B. (1998) Student Writing in Higher Education: an academic literacies approach. *Studies in Higher Education*, 23 (2), pp.157-172

Leathwood, C. and O'Connell, P. (2003) 'It's a struggle': the construction of the 'new student' in higher education' in *Journal of Education Policy*, 18(6):597-615

Lillis, T. M. (2001) *Student Writing: Access, Regulation and Desire*. London: Routledge

Lim, H. (2001), (2002), (2003) LEAP Survey, Unpublished report, Southampton Institute

Liu, Y. and Ginther, D. W. (2002) Instructional Strategies for Achieving a Positive Impression in Computer-Mediated Communication (CMC) Distance Education Courses. Proceedings of Teaching, Learning and Technology Conference, Middle Tennessee State University USA. http://www.mtsu.edu/~itconf/proceed01/8.html accessed Nov. 2005

Lowe, H. and Cook, A. (2003) Mind the Gap: are students prepared for higher education. *Journal of Further and Higher Education*, 27 (1), pp.53-76

Lublin, J. (1987) *Conducting Tutorials. Higher Education Research and Development*. Society of Australasia

Lyotard, J-F. (1984) *The postmodern condition: A report on knowledge*. Minneapolis: University of Minnesota Press.

Mager, J. (2003) 'Personalisation and Customisation – your keys to recruitment and success' Presentation at the National Student Retention Conference, San Diego. www.noellevitz.com accessed 4 November 2005

Malcolm, J. and Zukas, M. (2001) Bridging Pedagogic Gaps: conceptual discontinuities in higher education. *Teaching in Higher Education*, 6 (1), pp.33-42

Margolis, E. (ed.) (2001) *The Hidden Curriculum in Higher Education*. London: Routledge

Marr, L. and Leach B. (2005) What are we doing this for? Widening participation, employability and doing sociology. *LATISS – Learning and Teaching in the Social Sciences* 2 (1), pp.25-38

Marr, L. and Willmott L. (2004) Working Together: A Faculty-Wide Retention Strategy. Paper given at Staying Power, Supporting Students Retention and Success, University of Teesside, July

Maslow, A. (1954) *Motivation and Personality,* New York: Harper and Bros

Mason, R. and Weller M. (2000) Factors Affecting Students' Satisfaction on a Web Course. *Australian Journal of Educational Technology* 16(2), pp 173-2 http://www.ascilite.org.au/ajet/ajet16/mason.html accessed Dec 2005

McCartan, A. (2000) Use of IT in a Postgraduate Distance Learning Course: Part 2: Staff Perspectives. *Innovations in Education and Training International.* Routledge. 37(3) pp.192-198

McGill, I. and Beaty, L. (1995) *Action Learning: a guide for professional, management and educational development.* London: Kogan Page

Miller, C. and Blackman, C. (2004) *Learning during the first three years of post registration/post graduate employment.* The Linea Project. ERSC. University of Brighton/ University of Sussex at Brighton. http://www.sussex.ac.uk/usie/linea/index, accessed 11/3/06.

Morley, L. (1998) All you need is love: feminist pedagogy for empowerment and emotional labour in the academy. *International Journal of Inclusive Education,* 2 (1), pp.15-27

Murphy, M. and Fleming, T. (2000) Between common and college knowledge: exploring the boundaries between adult and higher education, *Studies in Continuing Education* 22(1):77-93

NATFHE (2005) Survey of University Lecturers Workload May 2005 http://www.natfhe.org.uk/?entityType=HTMLandid=494 accessed 12/12/05

National Audit Office (2002) *Improving student achievement in English higher education:* Report by the Comptroller and Auditor General, HC486, Session 2001-2002: 18 January 2002

Noble, J. (2004) *Student responses to early leaving* www.staffs.ac.uk/institutes/access/docs/28604uk2.doc, accessed 15/07/05

Oravec, J.A. (2000) Online Counselling and the Internet: Perspectives for mental health care supervision and education. *Journal of Mental Health* 9 (2), pp 121-135

Owen, M. (2002) 'Sometimes you feel you are in niche time': the personal tutor system, a case study. *Active Learning in Higher Education,* 3 (1), pp.7-23

Ozga, J. and Sukhnandan, L (1998) Undergraduate non-completion: Developing an explanatory model, *Higher Education Quarterly,* 53(3): 316-333.

Parker, S, Naylor, P. and Warmington, P. (2005) Widening participation in higher education: What can we learn from the ideologies and practices of committed practitioners? *Journal of Access Policy and Practice* 2(2)

Paulsen, M.F. (1998) Online Education: Pedagogical, Administrative and Technological Opportunities and Limitations. Presentation at RIBIE pp.1-10. http://home.nettskolen.nki.no/~morten/RIBIE accessed April, 2005

Phillips, R. (1994) Providing student support systems in project 2000 nurse education programmes – the personal tutor role of nurse teachers. *Nurse Education Today.* 14, pp216-222

Promnitz, J. and Germain, C. (1996) *Student Support Services and Academic Outcomes: Achieving Positive Outcomes.* Dept of Employment, Education, Training and Youth Affairs, Australia: Evaluations and Investigations Program, Higher Education Division. http://www.dest.gov.au/archive/highered/eippubs/student/eip96-10.htm accessed April, 2005

QAA (Quality Assurance Agency for Higher Education) (2004) Code of practice for the assurance of academic quality and standards in higher education. Section 2. Collaborative provision for flexible and distributed learning (including e-learning). QAA. http://www.qaa.ac.uk/academicinfrastructure/codeOfPractice/section2/default.asp accessed 6th January 2005

Quinn, J. (2004) Understanding working class 'drop-out' from higher education through a sociocultural lens: Cultural narratives and local contexts, *International Studies in Sociology of Education*, 14(1): 57-73.

Quinn, J., Thomas, L., Slack, K., Casey, L., Thexton, W. and Noble, J. (2005) *From life crisis to lifelong learning. Rethinking working-class 'drop out' from higher education*. York: Joseph Rowntree Foundation

Ramage, C. (2005) Analysis of the concept of 'hard work' as an experience of engaging in work based learning, in Rounce, K. and Workman, B. (eds) *Work-based learning in health care: applications and innovations*. Chichester: Kingsham Press.

Rana, R., Smith, E. and Walkling, J. (1999) *Degrees of Disturbance: the New Agenda*. Rugby: British Association for Counselling.

Read, B., Archer, A. and Leathwood, C. (2003) Challenging Cultures? Student Conceptions of 'Belonging' and 'Isolation' at a Post-1992 University, *Studies in Higher Education* 28(3): 261-277

Rekkedal, T. (1991) The Personal Tutor/Counsellor in Distance Education. Paper presented at the ZIFF-Ringkolloquium, FernUniversitat, Germany.pp1-9 http://www.nettskolen.com/forskning/25/ziffpers.htm accessed April, 2005

Rekkedal, T. (1997) *Training of distance tutors – A case from the NKI Foundation*, Norway. http://www.nettskolen.com/forskning/32/icde97.htm accessed April, 2005

Retention Team (2005) *Retaining non-traditional students in higher education*. Centre for Learning and Quality Enhancement: University of Teesside

Richardson, R. (1987) The role of personal tutor in nurse education: towards an understanding of practice in a college of nursing and midwifery at a particular point in time. *Journal of Advanced Nursing*. 27. pp614-621

Riddell, S., Tinklin, T. and Wilson, A. (2005) *Disabled Students in Higher Education*. Oxford: Routledge

Robbins Report (1963) *Higher Education: The Report of the Committee appointed by the Prime Minister under the Chairmanship of Lord Robbins 1961-63*, London: HMSO

Robinson, A. (2002) A Student Support Network, Academic Board Paper 02/AB/30, Southampton Institute

Robson, J. (1998) *Active Teaching and Learning*, http://www.gre.ac.uk/~bj61/talessi/atl.html, accessed 23 October 2001

Robson D. and Robson, M. (2000) Ethical issues in internet counselling. *Counselling Psychology Quarterly*. Taylor and Francis, pp249-257

Rogers, C. (1983) *Freedom to learn for the 80s*. New York: Macmillan Publishing Press

Romiszowski A. and Mason, R. (2002) Computer-Mediated Communication in: Jonassen A.H. (ed) *Handbook of Research for Educational Communication and Technology*. 2nd ed. online. Chapter 15. Association for Educational Communication and Technology. www.aect.org/edtech/15 pdf accessed April, 2005

Salmon G. (2004) *E-Moderating: The Key to Teaching and Learning Online* (2nd ed.). London: Taylor and Francis

SENDA (2001) *Special Educational Needs and Disability Act 2001*. London: Her Majesty's Stationery Office

Simpson, O. (1977) 'Post foundation Counselling': *Teaching At A Distance* 9 pp60-67.

Simpson, O. (2002) *Supporting Students in Online Open and Distance Learning*. London: RoutledgeFalmer

Simpson, O. (2003) *Student Retention in Online Open and Distance Learning*. London: RoutledgeFalmer

Simpson, O. (2004) The impact on retention of interventions to support distance students. *Open Learning*, 19 (1).

Simpson, O. (tbp 2006) The costs and benefits of student retention for students, institutions, and governments. *Studies in Learning, Evaluation, Innovation and Development* (Australia)

Sinclair, H. and Dale, L. (2000) The effect of student tuition fees on the diversity of intake within a Scottish new university. Paper presented at British Educational Research Association Annual Conference, 7-9 September 2000, Cardiff University

Snyder, C. and Shane J. Lopez (eds) (2001) *Handbook of Positive Psychology.* New York: Oxford University Press

Sosabowski, M.H, Bratt, A.M, Herson, K, Olivier G.W.J, Sawers, R. Taylor, S, Zahoui, A.-M, Denyer S.P. (2003) Enhancing Quality in the M.Pharm Degree Programme: Optimisation of the Personal Tutor System. *Pharmacy Education* Vol 3 (2) pp.103-108

Strathern, M. (2000) The Tyranny of Transparency. *British Educational Research Journal*, 26 (3), pp.309-321

Strauss, A. and Corbin, J. (1997) *Grounded Theory in Practice*. London: Sage Publications Inc.

Susan, C. and Williams, J. (2002) The reluctant workforce: undergraduates' part-time employment, *Journal of Education and Training* 44(1): 5-10

Swainson, M. (1977) The Spirit of Counsel. The Story of a Pioneer in Student Counselling. London: Neville Spearman.

Thomas, L. (2002) Student retention in higher education: The role of institutional habitus. *Journal Education Policy*, 17 (4), pp.423-442

Thomas, L., Quinn, J., Slack, K. and Casey, L. (2002) *Student services: Effective approaches to retaining students in higher education*. Stoke-on-Trent: Institute for Access Studies, Staffordshire University.

Tinto, V. (1975) Dropout from Higher Education: a theoretical synthesis of recent research *Review of Educational Research* 45 pp 89-125

Tinto, V. (1993) *Leaving College: rethinking the causes and cures of student attrition*, 2nd edition, Chicago: University of Chicago Press

Trowler, P., Fanghanel, J. and Wareham, T. (2005) Freeing the chi of change: the Higher Education Academy and enhancing teaching and learning in higher education. *Studies in Higher Education*, 30 (4), pp.427-444

Universities and Colleges Admissions Service (UCAS) (2002) *Paving the way.* Cheltenham: UCAS

Universities UK (UUK) (2001) *Patterns of higher education institutions in the UK (the Ramsden Report)*. London: UUK

Universities UK (UUK) (2002) *Student Services – effective approaches to retaining students in HE*. London: UUK

University of Bath (2004) *Guidelines for personal tutors*, http://internal.bath.ac.uk/tutors/, accessed December 2005

University of East Anglia (UEA) (2005) *Review of the undergraduate student advising system at UEA*. Internal Report to the Senate of the University of East Anglia, March 2005.

Vygotsky, L.S. (1978) *Mind in society. The developing of psychological processes*. Cambridge.MA: Harvard University Press

Walker, I. and Zhu, Y. (2003) Education, earnings and productivity: recent UK evidence'. *Labour Market Trends* III (3)

Ward, R., Jackson, N. and Strivens, J. (2005) Progress Files: Are We Achieving Our Goal? Working paper presented at Personal Development Planning Day Conference, University of Manchester, 29th November

Warren, D. (2002) 'Curriculum Design in a Context of Widening Participation in Higher Education.' *Arts and Humanities in Higher Education* 1(1): 85-89

Watson, D. (2000) Managing in Higher Education: The 'Wicked Issues'. *Higher Education Quarterly*, 54 (1), pp.5-21

Watt, K. (1974) *The Titanic Effect: Planning for the Unthinkable*, New York: Sinauer Associates incorporated

Watts, A.G. (1999) *The Role of the Personal Adviser. Concepts and Issues.* Centre for Guidance Studies Occasional Paper. Derby: Centre for Guidance Studies.

Wenger, E. (1998) *Communities of Practice: Learning, meaning and identity.* Cambridge: Cambridge University Press

Wheeler, S. and Birtle, J. (1993) *A handbook for personal tutors.* Society for Research into Higher Education and Open University Press

Wiesenberg, F. (2001) The Roller Coaster Life of the Online Learner: How Distance Educators Can Help Students Cope. *Canadian Journal of University Continuing Education.* Vol 27, No. 2 pp.33-59

Wilcox, P., Winn, S. and Fyvie-Gauld, M. (2005) 'It was nothing to do with the university, it was just the people': the role of social support in the first-year experience of higher education'. *Studies in Higher Education* 30 (6), pp.707-722

Williamson, S. (2004) www.ltsneng.ac.uk/nef/events/first_year_belfast.asp, accessed May 2004

Winnicott, D. W. (1965) *The maturational process and the facilitative environment.* London: Hogarth Press

Woodley, A. (1987) Understanding Adult Student Dropout, in Thorpe, M. and Grugeon, D (eds) *Open Learning for Adults*, pp110-124. Harlow UK: Longman Open Learning

Wright T. (2005) Personal Tutor Conference, The Higher Education Academy, http://www.heacademy.ac.uk/3187.htm, accessed January 2006

Yorke, M. (1999) *Leaving Early: Undergraduate Non-completion in Higher Education.* London: Taylor and Francis

Yorke, M. (2000) The Quality of the Student Experience: what can institutions learn from data relating to non-completion? *Quality in Higher Education* 6 (1), pp.61-75

Yorke, M. (2002) Academic Failure: a Retrospective View from Non-completing Students, in Peelo, M. and Wareham, T. (eds) *Failing Students in Higher Education.* Buckingham: SRHE and Open University Press

Yorke, M. and Thomas, L. (2003) Improving the Retention of Students from Lower Socio-economic Groups. *Journal of Higher Education Policy and Management*, 25 (1), pp. 63-74

Zeithaml, V. A, Parasuraman, A. and Berry, L. L. (1990) *Delivering Quality Service: Balancing Customer Perceptions and Expectations*, New York: Free Press

Index